Impact!

WORKBOOK

Civic, Social and Political Education
for Junior Certificate

Fifth edition

Jeanne Barrett
and
Fiona Richardson

GILL EDUCATION

CSPE

Gill Education
Hume Avenue
Park West
Dublin 12
www.gilleducation.ie

Gill Education is an imprint of M.H. Gill & Co.

© Jeanne Barrett and Fiona Richardson 2010
Artwork by Peter Bull Art Studio, East Sussex, UK
Print Origination by Mike Connor Design and Illustration, UK

978 07171 4530 0

The paper used in this book is made from the wood pulp of managed
forests. For every tree felled, at least one tree is planted, thereby
renewing natural resources.

PHOTO CREDITS

For permission to reproduce photographs the author and publisher gratefully acknowledge the following:

'It's Time to Unite' Unite for Children, Unite against AIDS poster © UNICEF Canada: 122; © A. Gutman, International Committee of the Red Cross: 114TR; © Alamy: 3TR, 18CL, 24BT, 24CB, 25C, 25CT, 31, 3TL, 60B, 69B, 75B, 75TB; © ALONE: 80; © Amnesty International: 18C, © Amnesty International Ireland: 147B; © Arup: 62; © Bike Furniture Design: 27; © Corbis: 24T, 118B, 129, 137BL; © Crimestoppers: 87; © Earth Hour India: 40; © Earth Sciences for Society: 159; © European Communities: 75C, 102; © Fairtrade Mark Ireland: 119; © FAO: 105TB; © Fianna Fáil: 150BL, 150T; © Getty: 3BL ,3CL, 18BL, 19BL, 19BR, 19TL, 19TR, 25B, 33CB, 46TL, 108R, 118CT; © Give it a Swirl: 147T; © Green Party: 150B; © Imagefile: 3CR, 3CTL, 16, 24B, 24CT, 25T, 33B, 33T, 33TB, 46TR, 113, 118C, 157; © INSTRAW: 105CT; © International Committee of the Red Cross: 114; © International Federation of Red Cross and Red Crescent Societies: 114TC; © International Women's Day: 158T; © Japanese Red Cross: 114BR; © Magnum Photos: 60T; © Niall Mellon Township Trust: 148B; © Ombudsman for Children's Office: 161B; © Oxfam Ireland: 161T; © Panos: 33C, 106BCR, 106BL, 106TCL, 106TCR, 106TL, 106TR; © Photocall: 53, 73, 137T; © Photolibrary: 18TL, 19CL, 24C, 33BT, 74T; © Press Association: 69T; © Reuters: 110R, 118CB, 137C; © Rex: 118T; © Self Help Africa: 162B; © The Irish Times: 74B, 75T, 137B, 150C; © TopFoto: 18CBL; © Trocaire/Kim Haughton: 110L; © UN: 103; © UN Photo: 13; © UN Photo/Eric Kanalstein: 106BCL; © UN Photo/Paulo Filgueiras: 108L; © UNDP: 105T; © UNEP: 105B; © UNHCR: 112; © UNHCR: 105CB; © UNICEF: 105C; © Wrexham College: 116T; Courtesy of Barnardos: 77; Courtesy of Camara: 127; Courtesy of chewitbinit.com: 162T; Courtesy of Concern: 123; Courtesy of Irish Red Cross © André Corvin: 114TL; Courtesy of Longford Co. Council: 50; Courtesy of Oxfam: 125; Courtesy of Patrick Maphoso: 52; Courtesy of the Houses of the Oireachtas: 68; Courtesy of the Irish Traveller Movement: 15, 79L, 79R; Courtesy of the National Anti-Racism Awareness Programme: 116B; Courtesy of Wikimedia Commons: 148T, 158B.

The author and publisher have made every effort to trace all copyright holders, but if any have been inadvertently overlooked we would be pleased to make the necessary arrangement at the first opportunity.

CONTENTS

Sample Exam Papers

Chapter 1

EXERCISE 1 SURVIVAL ISLAND

We must have certain needs met in order to survive. What would you bring to this desert island to help you survive?

1. Choose four items written on the suitcases and write your choices in the blank suitcases.

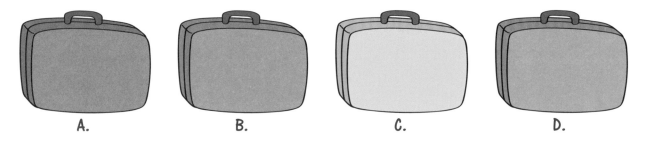

A.   B.   C.   D.

2. Explain the reasons for your choices.

Reason A:

_____

_____

Reason B:

_____

_____

Reason C:

_____

_____

Reason D:

_____

_____

3. What is the difference between a want and a need? Explain your answer.

_____

_____

EXERCISE 2 THE RIGHTS PICTURE

The United Nations Declaration of Human Rights names rights that every person should have. Below is a list of some of those rights.

1. Match the rights with the pictures by filling in the number beside the corresponding photo. Two rights are named but have no pictures. Draw pictures to match these rights.

a)  ☐

e)  ☐

b)  ☐

f)  ☐

c)  ☐

g)  i

d)  ☐

h)  v

i)   The right to leisure and rest

ii)   The right to marry

iii) The right to have food

iv) The right to health care

v)   The right to an education

vi) The right to equal treatment before the courts

vii) The right to vote

viii) The right to shelter

2. Name another set of rights drawn up by the United Nations.

EXERCISE 3 CHILDREN'S RIGHTS

Look at the United Nations Convention on the Rights of the Child. These rights are separated into four main areas.

DEVELOPMENT RIGHTS
Play
Education
Cultural activities
To speak your own language

SURVIVAL RIGHTS
Food
Clean water
Shelter
Medicine/health care

UN CONVENTION ON THE RIGHTS OF THE CHILD

PARTICIPATION RIGHTS
To take an active part in society
To express your opinion
To meet together and express your views

PROTECTION RIGHTS
To be kept safe and not be hurt
Not to be used as cheap labour
Not to be used as a child soldier

1. In each of the four areas named above, circle the right you think is most important.

2. Draw a picture of each right you have chosen and explain why it is important.

a) Development Right

This right is important because

_____

_____

_____

_____

_____

_____

_____

_____

_____

b) Survival Right

This right is important because

_____

_____

_____

_____

_____

_____

_____

_____

_____

RIGHTS AND RESPONSIBILITIES

c) **Participation Right**

This right is important because

_____

_____

_____

_____

_____

_____

_____

_____

_____

d) **Protection Right**

This right is important because

_____

_____

_____

_____

_____

_____

_____

_____

_____

EXERCISE 4   HAND IN HAND

Having rights also means having responsibilities.

Example: Everyone has the right to a clean environment and each of us is responsible for not littering or damaging our world.

1.   In the arms below, fill in the missing right or the missing responsibility.

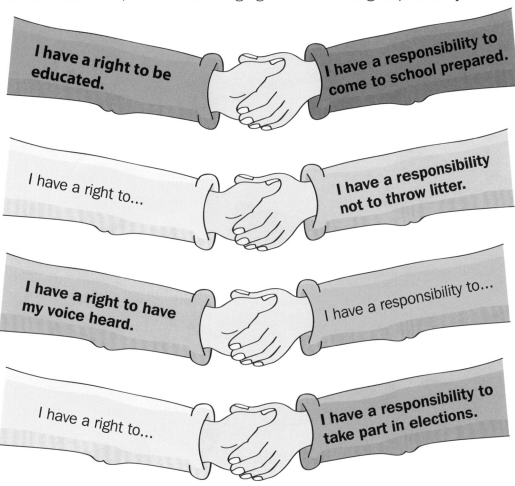

I have a right to be educated.

I have a responsibility to come to school prepared.

I have a right to…

I have a responsibility not to throw litter.

I have a right to have my voice heard.

I have a responsibility to…

I have a right to…

I have a responsibility to take part in elections.

2.   Name **two** rights you think are important and the responsibility that goes with each right.

I have a right to…

I have a responsibility to…

I have a right to…

I have a responsibility to…

EXERCISE 5 POSITIVE OR NOT?

Being a member of a school community means that you have responsibilities as well as rights.

1. On the signs below, use a **green** pen to circle the actions you think are **positive** and a **red** pen to circle the actions you think would **not** be OK.

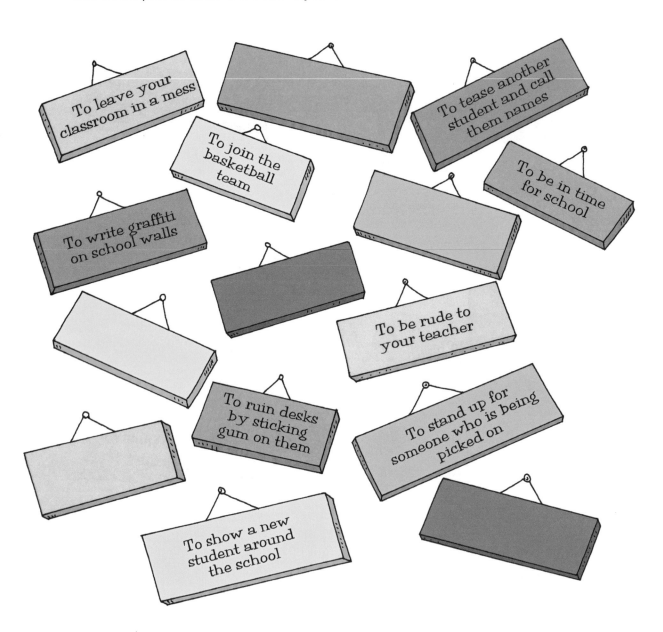

2. In the blank signs, write some actions that would show you are a responsible student.

3. Explain why you think schools have rules about some of the actions you have circled in red.

_____

_____

EXERCISE 6 BULLYING – NO WAY!

There are different kinds of bullying. Read the story below to see why going to school became difficult for this student.

I hate school. I hate all the teachers. I hate all the girls. I particularly hate Maria and Alice. They raise their eyebrows and then splutter with laughter whenever I go near them. The other girls have started doing it too. And everyone groans whenever I answer in class. I can't help knowing lots. What's so bad about being clever? I wish I didn't have to go to school. Maybe I'll bunk off and creep back home and hide in the attic all day like a real Anne Frank.

Extract from Jacqueline Wilson's novel *Secrets*

1. Why do you think this girl hates school and everyone in it?

   _____

   _____

2. In this story, what kind of bullying is being carried out?

   _____

   _____

3. Why does this student feel that she is being picked on?

   _____

   _____

4. How does the girl in the story deal with the bullying?

   _____

   _____

5. Suggest another way of dealing with this problem.

   _____

   _____

6. Do you think this girl is being denied any of her rights?

   _____

   _____

EXERCISE 7 YOUR ADVICE

Imagine you have been asked to design an anti-bullying web page for your school.

1. Design a home page and slogan for your anti-bullying web page. You could include your school name and crest.

Anti-Bullying Web Page

2. Your web page should contain information on the kinds of bullying behaviour that are not acceptable in your school. Make a list of some of the things that could be seen as bullying behaviour. Use the words in the box below to help you with your answer.

> spreading rumours   online gossiping   name-calling
>
> teasing   saying nasty things   writing nasty things
>
> sending mean text messages   ignoring the person
>
> leaving the person out

Bullying behaviour can be:

- _____
- _____
- _____
- _____
- _____

3. Give some advice on what to do if you see bullying going on.

If you see bullying going on . . .

- **Refuse to join in.**
- _____
- _____
- _____
- _____
- _____

4. Give some advice on what to do if you are being bullied online.

If you are being bullied online . . .

- **Tell a teacher.**
- _____
- _____
- _____
- _____
- _____

EXERCISE 8 WHO DOES WHAT?

There are many organisations that support and raise awareness of the rights of others in society.

1. Using the table below, match the organisations listed with the issue that concerns them. There may be more than one organisation concerned with the same issue.

Organisations

A. Focus Ireland

B. ActionAid Ireland

C. Age Action Ireland

D. Alone

E. Barnardos

F. Concern Worldwide

G. Goal

H. Irish Red Cross Society

I. Irish Refugee Council

J. Simon Community

K. UNICEF

L. Salvation Army

M. Trócaire

N. St Vincent de Paul

O. Irish Society for the Prevention of Cruelty to Animals

P. Voice

Q. Irish Wildlife Trust

R. Lion's Club

S. Irish Society for the Prevention of Cruelty to Children

Concern/Issue	Organisation
1. Homelessness	A , J
2. Refugees	
3. The developing world	
4. Poverty in Irish society	
5. The needs of the elderly	
6. Care of the environment	
7. Child welfare	
8. Animal welfare	

EXERCISE 9 HUMAN RIGHTS BEGIN AT HOME

Eleanor Roosevelt, the wife of the American President Franklin D. Roosevelt, was the Chairperson of the Commission on Human Rights, which was responsible for writing the United Nations Declaration of Human Rights. She was passionate about trying to encourage everyone to take up the cause of human rights. She felt people should see that defending human rights is not just about taking action about bad things happening somewhere else in the world: we should also be aware of what is happening on our own doorstep. She believed that the fate of human rights lay in the hands of all citizens in all our communities.

Read the following quotation and answer the questions below.

Where, after all, do universal human rights begin? In small places, close to home – so close and so small that they cannot be seen on any maps of the world. Yet they are the world of the individual person; the neighbourhood he lives in; the school or college he attends; the factory, farm, or office where he works. Such are the places where every man, woman, and child seeks equal justice, equal opportunity, equal dignity without discrimination. Unless these rights have meaning there, they have little meaning anywhere. Without concerted citizen action to uphold them close to home, we shall look in vain for progress in the larger world.

Eleanor Roosevelt

1. Where did Eleanor Roosevelt believe that human rights begin?

   _____

   _____

   _____

2. What did she believe would happen if we did not take citizen action close to home?

   _____

   _____

   _____

   _____

3. Can you name any groups or organisations in your school that are concerned about human rights?

   _____

   _____

   _____

4. Can you name any organisations in your local community that look out for people's human rights?

   _____

   _____

   _____

5. Do you consider it important to look out for the human rights of others? Explain your answer.

   _____

   _____

   _____

   _____

EXERCISE 10 DISCRIMINATION ON YOUR DOORSTEP

Read the following piece by an Irish Traveller, Nellie Joyce, about the life of a Traveller, and answer the questions below.

Travelling means my whole life. I like everything about it. Travellers are committed to their families, we all help one another. The travelling life has changed a lot – the tents and wagons are gone and we're all in trailers and on sites or in schemes of houses. Travellers in houses want to be called a Traveller; we'll always be Travellers. A lot can live and pass as settled people, but there's not many that'll deny they're Travellers. We always knew what we were and told the kids what they were. Kids are now called knackers and they didn't know what it was and were getting confused. We don't call you a president or politician or the name of the trade you might have, why call us a knacker? I can't understand it, we're not treated like normal Irish people.

Nellie Joyce, Blanchardstown
(Source: Pavee Point website)

1. How has 'travelling life' changed?

   _____

   _____

   _____

2. Name two ways in which Travellers are discriminated against.

   a) _____

   b) _____

3. Name three other groups in society that are sometimes discriminated against.

   a) _____

   b) _____

   c) _____

4. Choose **one** of the groups you named above and say what human rights they are being denied.

   _____

   _____

RIGHTS AND RESPONSIBILITIES / HUMAN DIGNITY

EXERCISE 11 GANDHI

We all have a responsibility to look out for the rights of others. When we do this we are also protecting our own rights. Read the story below of one man, Gandhi, who campaigned on behalf of his people, and answer the questions that follow.

Mahatma Gandhi

Mahatma Gandhi (1869–1948) was born in India and studied law in England. After working as a lawyer for a short time in India, he went to live in South Africa. He discovered that Indians were treated very badly there. So he began to campaign for their rights. Even though he was against violence of any kind and his protest was always peaceful, he was in prison many times. Eventually, because of his campaigns Indians were given some new rights.

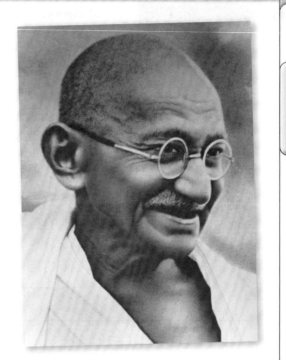

When he returned from South Africa he became involved in India's struggle for independence from England. Again, he approved of only peaceful protest, such as asking people not to buy British goods and holding sit-down protests on the streets of India. Gandhi himself often used fasting as a method of protest. He hoped that such methods would show the English that using violence against his fellow Indians would not keep them down or break their spirit. Gandhi said, 'the trouble with an eye for an eye is that it leaves the whole world blind'. In 1947, as a result of all these actions, India became an independent country.

Another great campaign in Gandhi's life was against the caste system in India. (A caste is a social level or class.) Under this system a person is born into a specific caste and may never leave it. The lowest class was called the 'untouchables'. These people lived in terrible poverty. Again, his peaceful campaigns on behalf of the 'untouchables' had good results and the lives of many Indians were improved.

Gandhi continued his peaceful campaigns until he was assassinated by a Hindu fanatic in 1948.

1. Name **three** different campaigns that Gandhi was involved in.

   a) _____

   b) _____

   c) _____

2. Name **three** different forms of protest that Gandhi used.

   a) _____

   b) _____

   c) _____

3. What do you understand by Gandhi's words, **'the trouble with an eye for an eye is that it makes the whole world blind'**?

   _____

   _____

   _____

4. Name the American civil rights leader who was inspired by Gandhi's methods of non-violent protest (check back in your *Impact!* textbook).

   _____

5. Name another method of peaceful protest not mentioned in Gandhi's story.

   _____

6. If you were involved in a human rights campaign, which method of peaceful protest do you think would be most effective? Why?

   _____

   _____

   _____

   _____

EXERCISE 12 PEOPLE FOR PEACE

Alfred Nobel was born in Sweden in 1833. Nobel invented dynamite and later built many companies all over the world. In his will he asked that his fortune be used to give prizes to those who have done their best in areas such as peace, medicine and literature.

The Nobel Peace Prize is awarded each year to individuals and organisations who work in the area of peace and human rights.

1. Draw a line to match the person, or the logo of the organisation, with the description of the work for which they won the Nobel Peace Prize.

This organisation won for their worldwide work for the protection of the rights of prisoners of conscience.

This man won for his campaign for civil rights in America.

This man won for setting up the 'Village Bank', which has given small loans to over seven million Bangladeshis, 97% of whom have been women.

This woman won for her work with the poor around the world.

These men won for their work to end apartheid and bring peace to South Africa.

EXERCISE 13 WHAT DOES BEING A GOOD CITIZEN MEAN?

Read what some students have said being a good citizen means.

I think being a good citizen means not breaking the law.

I think being a good citizen means not throwing litter.

I think a good citizen is someone who never steals from other students' lockers.

I think a good citizen is someone who raises money for different causes.

I think a good citizen is someone who gets involved in their community.

What does being a good citizen mean to you? Write your answers in the speech bubbles below.

I think a good citizen is

_____

_____

_____

I think a good citizen is

_____

_____

_____

I think a good citizen is

_____

_____

_____

I think a good citizen is

_____

_____

_____

EXERCISE 14 BUILDING CITIZEN BLOCKS

Written on the blocks are ways in which you could become an active citizen, and ways in which you would not be an active citizen.

You join a club in your community	You decide it's too much trouble to return your library books			You decide to visit an elderly neighbour
You always look for 'Fairtrade' goods in the supermarket	You don't bother to vote in the student council election	You take part in a fun run for a local charity		
	You pass up on the chance to go to a fundraising event for 'Concern'		You join a political party	
You get involved in an anti-racist campaign in school	You decide it's too much trouble to recycle stuff		You always leave the lights and TV on when you go out	
	You decide to show a new student round the school	You pass up the chance to become a member of the Junior Amnesty International group in school	You join the 'Clean up the Park' campaign in your area	
		You join the 'Green Committee' in school		You decide you won't register to vote when you are 18.

1. Use **green** to colour all the bricks that would help you become an active citizen.

2. Use **red** to colour all the bricks that would mean you are **not** becoming an active citizen.

3. Choose four **good citizenship actions** from the wall above and rank them in order of importance from (a) to (d).

    a) _____

    b) _____

    c) _____

    d) _____

4. In the blank bricks add your own ideas on how to become an active citizen or not.

EXERCISE 15 REVISION

Rights and Responsibilities Word Search

D	D	N	Y	R	H	Y	Y	Z	P	C	F	E	F	H
C	E	K	O	U	I	T	D	R	N	O	L	J	Q	O
R	E	C	M	I	S	G	O	X	E	N	C	L	Z	I
M	N	A	L	E	N	T	H	G	E	V	C	P	J	O
F	N	O	N	A	E	I	P	T	D	E	Y	A	L	P
P	X	M	E	C	R	X	P	L	S	N	L	A	G	R
H	A	J	T	E	K	A	W	O	Q	T	K	W	N	W
L	R	I	K	F	M	S	T	C	Y	I	E	F	Y	T
A	O	D	Z	H	Q	Y	B	I	X	O	S	N	I	C
N	L	A	V	I	V	R	U	S	O	N	N	Q	B	L
Q	P	T	G	V	F	M	H	H	J	N	O	L	I	R
D	Y	S	Y	C	S	R	O	Z	G	Z	I	H	G	O
V	O	H	F	Z	E	N	J	D	B	A	T	J	P	J
H	K	F	R	F	L	J	U	G	J	O	A	K	D	R
W	F	Q	U	N	I	T	E	D	V	A	N	H	G	M

Find these words in the grid above.

AMNESTY	CONVENTION	SURVIVAL
HUMAN	UNITED	DECLARATION
RIGHTS	NATIONS	NEEDS
OPINION	PLAY	PROTECTION

Word Grid

Use the clues below to fill in the word grid.

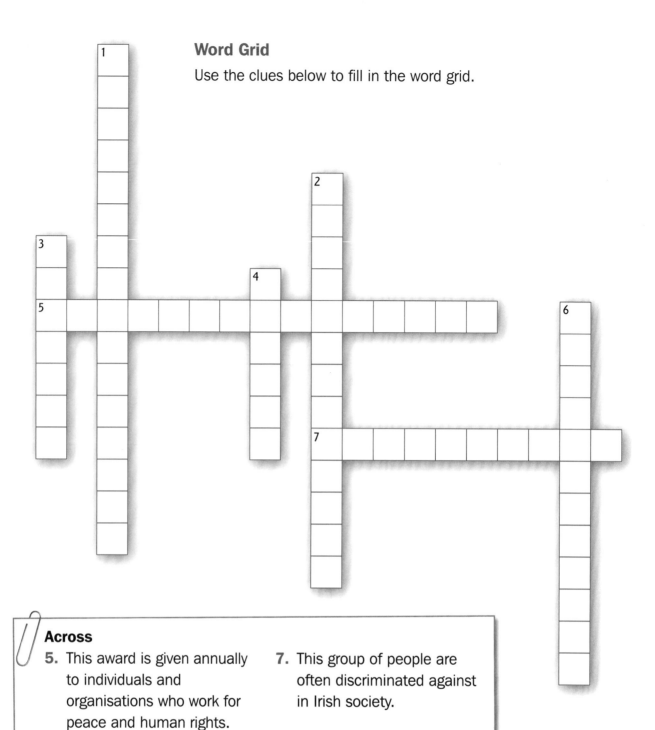

Across

5. This award is given annually to individuals and organisations who work for peace and human rights.

7. This group of people are often discriminated against in Irish society.

Down

1. These go hand in hand with rights.

2. This organisation drew up the Convention on the Rights of the Child.

3. This organisation works for rights around the world.

4. This man campaigned for rights in India.

6. If you treat one person less favourably than another because of their racial or ethnic origin, you do this.

Chapter 2

EXERCISE 16 HOW GREEN ARE YOU?

Answer the quiz by putting a circle around Always, Sometimes or Never.

1. Do you take a shower instead of a bath?

Always

Sometimes

Never

2. Do you recycle cans and bottles?

Always

Sometimes

Never

3. Do you walk or cycle to school?

Always

Sometimes

Never

4. Do you turn the tap off when washing your teeth?

Always

Sometimes

Never

5. Do you turn off the lights/TV/CD player when you are the last in a room?

Always

Sometimes

Never

6. Do you use recycled paper?

Always

Sometimes

Never

7. Do you use litter bins?

Always

Sometimes

Never

8. Do you bring a bag with you to the shops?

Always

Sometimes

Never

9. Do you only turn the washing machine on when it is full?

Always

Sometimes

Never

10. Do you use environmentally friendly deodorants?

Always

Sometimes

Never

Add up the number of times you have circled each word to find out how green you are.

So How Green are You?

◀ ▶ ⊗ 🏠

Mainly Always:
Well, you are definitely green. Well done, and keep up the good work.

Score: _____

Mainly Sometimes:
Getting green, but there is more you could do.

Score: _____

Mainly Never:
You have a long way to go – start today.

Score: _____

EXERCISE 17 DON'T JUST DUMP IT!

One way to cut down on the amount of waste we produce is to:

Reduce - Reuse - Recycle - Repair

1. This dump contains many items that can be reused, recycled or repaired. Draw a line linking each item in the dump to the bin it belongs in.

2. Name two items not in the dump that could be reused, recycled or repaired.

   a) _____

   b) _____

3. Suggest some ways in which your school could reduce, reuse and recycle.

   _____

   _____

   _____

EXERCISE 18 REINVENT

About 75% of the rubbish we create can be reused or recycled. So we need to think carefully about every item of rubbish we produce. How can you reuse your own rubbish? If you have outgrown your favourite toy, DVD or PlayStation game, a charity shop or children's hospital might be very glad to have them. In the developing world people are much more likely to be inventive and reuse items, often for a new or different purpose. For example, in Africa and Asia old rubber tyres are cut up and reshaped to be used as rubber soles for shoes.

A chair made from recycled bicycle wheels

In groups, see how many ideas you can come up with for reusing the following items.

1. Plastic containers could be used again as/for: _____

_____

2. Glass coffee jars could be used again as/for: _____

_____

3. Cardboard boxes could be used again as/for: _____

_____

4. Vegetable and fruit peelings could be used again as/for: _____

_____

5. Old newspapers could be used again as/for: _____

_____

6. Old clothes could be used again as/for: _____

_____

7. Pasta shells/tubes that have gone out of date could be used as/for: _____

_____

8. _____ could be used as/for: _____

_____

9. _____ could be used as/for: _____

_____

10. _____ could be used as/for: _____

_____

EXERCISE 19 POWER OF ONE

There are lots of ways to help you use less water, less electricity and less petrol, and to reduce your impact on the world's resources. For example, about one third of the average family's water comes from flushing loos, which uses about 12 litres of water per flush. By putting a water-filled plastic tub or a brick in the toilet cistern you could save over 3,000 litres of water every year.

The Power of One campaign shows us how the actions of each individual can make a difference in our homes, schools, offices, etc. Read the following extract from the Power of One brochure and see how you can reduce energy use in your bedroom.

The Power of One

A few simple steps will keep bedrooms warm and cosy without wasting energy.

- If you use an electric blanket, switch it on no more than half an hour before you go to bed and switch off just before you get into bed.

- Heat bedrooms to 18 °C or less and make sure you turn off the heat when you're not there. Keep the curtains closed at night and make sure you don't just heat the space between the curtains and the window. A radiator shelf can also deflect the convection currents past the curtains into the room.

- Remember to check if phone chargers are left plugged in. Even if they're not in use they still use energy.

- If you see little red lights before you nod off for the night, that means the TV or DVD player is on standby and still using electricity.

- Unplug radio alarm clocks when you get up in the morning – they waste energy during the day if left switched on.

(Taken from the Power of One campaign.)

In groups, make up a list of your top tips for saving energy and using less water and electricity in your home or school:

The Power of One

TOP TEN TIPS!

1. _____
   _____

2. _____
   _____

3. _____
   _____

4. _____
   _____

5. _____
   _____

6. _____
   _____

7. _____
   _____

8. _____
   _____

9. _____
   _____

10. _____
    _____

EXERCISE 20 GREEN ENERGY

Coal, gas, oil and peat are the main sources of energy in Ireland. These are non-renewable sources of energy and will one day run out.

The blades of the windmill name sources of 'green energy'. Green energy is made from renewable energy sources.

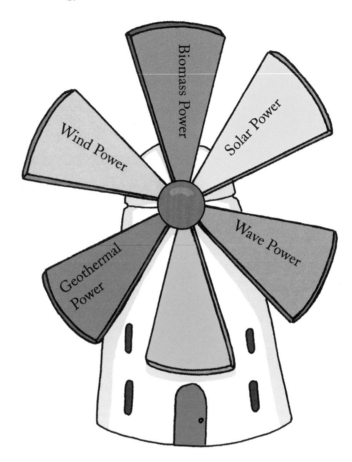

1. Use the 'green energy' sources from the windmill to complete the following sentences.

    a) **Energy made by taking heat from the sun is called**

        _____ _____.

    b) **We can take energy from plants: for example, in Brazil sugar cane is made into fuel for cars. This kind of energy is called**

        _____ _____.

    c) **Waves can be used to push air or water to make electricity. This energy is called**

        _____ _____.

    d) **Using the wind to create energy is called**

        _____ _____.

    e) **Using heat from the earth's core to make energy is called**

        _____ _____.

EXERCISE 21 GOING GREEN

Read the following newspaper article and answer the questions that follow.

2020 target for 350,000 electric cars

A target of 350,000 electric vehicles on Irish roads and no petrol or diesel cars on sale by 2020 was set out yesterday by an Oireachtas energy committee, writes Paddy Comyn.

A new report from the Oireachtas Joint Committee on Climate Change and Energy Security recommends targets whereby all new cars on sale by 2020 would have electric engines, with at least 350,000 electric vehicles in use by that year, 100,000 more than the target already set by the Government.

By 2016, the committee wants 100,000 privately-operated battery electric vehicles on Irish roads. No petrol or diesel engines will be sold as new cars by 2020 – the difference between running them and running electric vehicles will be so vast there will be no demand, said the report's author, Fine Gael TD Simon Coveney.

'We recognise that targets are being set, but we are asking the Government to be more ambitious and more proactive in the infrastructure required to make that happen,' he said.

'This is the biggest carbon-reduction initiative under consideration by Government, bar none.' . . .

The report doesn't go into specifics on incentives for buyers and it notes that the success of electric vehicles depends in part on manufacturers ramping up production of both batteries and vehicles and the presence of the proper infrastructure.

The committee has met with Better Place, a start-up led by former SAP executive Shai Agassi. The Better Place model is that the battery, which makes up a major cost of an electric vehicle, would be treated separately to the car. Buyers would lease the battery and buy kilometres, just like minutes are bought from a mobile phone company.

This would not only keep the cost down, but would also address the issue of the short range of such vehicles. A purpose-built swapping station would allow users to swap batteries. Pilot programmes of Better Place are being rolled out in Israel, Denmark and Japan.

The committee pointed out that Ireland is suited to the rollout of electric vehicles by virtue of its size, the fact that it is an island nation ...

(Irish Times)

1. How many electric cars does the Oireachtas energy committee want to see on Irish roads by 2020?

_____

2. What is the Better Place model and how does it work?

_____

_____

_____

3. Why would Ireland be suitable for electric cars?

_____

_____

_____

4. Design a poster advertising the benefits of driving an electric car.

EXERCISE 22 RAINFORESTS

Tropical rainforests once covered over 14% of the earth's land surface; now rainforests cover less than 6%. Rainforests are disappearing at the rate of 80 acres per minute. In the exercise below, match the reasons why some people want to continue to cut down the rainforests and others are against it. Draw a line matching the person to the reason.

I need to clear the trees to make way for building houses and shopping centres.

I need to stop rainforests being cut down because the plants can be used for medical research.

The rainforests cannot be cut down as myself and my family will have nowhere to live.

The rainforests are needed to suck up all the CO_2 and pollutants.

Stop cutting down the trees or my habitat will be destroyed and I will have nowhere to live.

I need to clear trees to make more places for cattle to graze.

1. What do you think is the strongest reason for not cutting down the rainforests? Give two explanations for your answer.

Reason: _____

Explanation 1: _____

_____

_____

Explanation 2: _____

_____

_____

2. What do you think is the strongest reason for cutting down the rainforests? Give two explanations for your answer.

Reason: _____

Explanation 1: _____

_____

_____

Explanation 2: _____

_____

_____

3. What two actions could you take to raise awareness about the importance of the rainforests?

Action 1: _____

_____

_____

Action 2: _____

_____

_____

4. Design a poster to show why the rainforests are important for everyone.

EXERCISE 23 GET THE PICTURE!

Study this cartoon on environmental problems facing Ireland today and answer the questions that follow.

1. Looking through the window of this minister's office, can you see two causes of CO_2 (carbon dioxide) pollution?

   a) _____

   b) _____

2. What is the Kyoto Agreement trying to achieve?

   _____

   _____

   _____

   _____

   _____

3. Under the Kyoto Agreement, if Ireland does not reduce its production of greenhouse gases, what will happen?

   _____

   _____

   _____

   _____

4. What other greenhouse gas is mentioned in the report on the minister's desk?

_____

_____

_____

5. Where, according to the report, is this gas produced?

_____

_____

_____

6. What three things in this minister's office show concern about the environment?

a) _____

b) _____

c) _____

7. What would you put on this minister's 'To Do' list to help cut down on greenhouse gases and improve the environment in Ireland?

_____

_____

_____

8. What CSPE concept can you come up with by adding six letters to this minister's name?

S ___ ___ ___ ___ ___ ___ SHIP

9. In December 2009 there was a huge environmental conference to discuss follow-on actions to the Kyoto Agreement. In which city was this conference held?

_____

EXERCISE 24 BIRTHDAY WISHES

Imagine it is the earth's birthday today. It is 46 years old. This is its life story so far. Using the pictures below, see if you can write the sections of the earth's life story that are missing. Sections 1 and 6 have been done already.

1. Not much is known about the earth aged 0–41 years old.

2. At age 42 you can see on the earth . . .

    _____

    _____

    _____

    _____

3. At age 43 you can see on the earth . . .

    _____

    _____

    _____

    _____

    _____

4. At age **44** you can see on the earth . . .

_____

_____

_____

_____

_____

5. At age **45** you can see on the earth . . .

_____

_____

_____

_____

_____

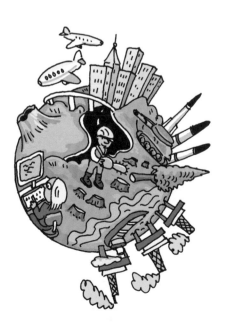

6. In the last minute, just before the earth was **46** years old, human beings have caused the destruction of many hundreds of animals. We have used up many of the world's resources. We have weapons that can destroy the earth in seconds. All this has happened in the last minute of the world's imagined **46** years.

EXERCISE 25 EARTH HOUR

Earth Hour is an event that takes place around the world to raise awareness about the importance of our environment. It takes place on 28 March every year.

Examine the poster for Earth Hour and answer the questions that follow.

1. In what country was this advert used to highlight Earth Hour? _____

2. How many countries take part in Earth Hour? _____

3. Suggest three activities that the following groups could organise to support the event.

a) A local neighbourhood: _____

_____

_____

b) A local business: _____

_____

_____

c) A family: _____

_____

_____

4. Imagine that, as part of learning about stewardship of the environment, your CSPE class has decided to celebrate Earth Hour. Draw a sketch of a poster that you would use to raise awareness about the event. You should include a suitable slogan in your sketch, with a drawing or picture.

EXERCISE 26 REVISION

Environment Word Search

S	S	U	W	U	C	N	C	C	D	E	R	R	O	R
F	I	T	F	L	Y	E	A	O	N	P	E	E	T	T
P	I	H	S	D	R	A	W	E	T	S	D	W	O	V
O	P	V	X	E	S	E	R	N	R	W	U	O	Y	Z
Y	B	W	O	X	R	G	P	E	M	Z	C	P	X	N
N	H	U	L	S	Y	O	W	A	D	L	E	R	G	G
W	J	G	C	A	B	O	F	N	I	V	S	A	L	E
W	Y	C	T	X	P	S	G	N	E	R	Y	L	I	K
Z	V	W	P	D	P	I	L	Y	I	E	T	O	S	B
Y	K	C	N	E	S	U	E	R	F	A	R	S	U	G
I	G	I	R	E	C	Y	C	L	E	X	R	G	O	X
H	W	N	S	O	D	U	R	Q	P	Y	D	X	X	P
I	W	R	T	W	U	S	K	T	N	J	B	B	E	D
Z	F	H	F	X	B	O	T	O	Y	K	Q	S	Y	Z
K	M	T	O	Q	O	F	I	F	P	H	T	I	L	E

Find these words in the grid above. ◀ ▶ ⊗ ⌂

ENERGY	GREEN	KYOTO
RAINFORESTS	RECYCLE	REDUCE
REPAIR	REUSE	SOLAR POWER
STEWARDSHIP	WIND POWER	

Environment Word Grid

Use the clues below to fill in the word grid

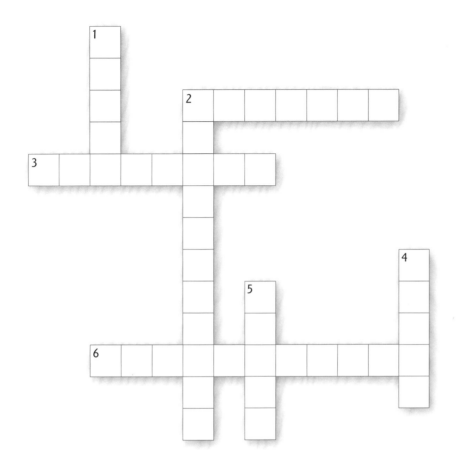

Across

2. You can do this with paper and glass bottles.
3. A place where rubbish is dumped.
6. These are not renewable sources of energy.

Down

1. Wind, wave and sun are examples of this kind of energy.
2. These are being cut down at the rate of 80 acres per minute.
4. When you bring your own shopping bag you do this.
5. This energy is made from taking heat from the sun.

Chapter 3

EXERCISE 27 WHAT IS A COMMUNITY?

1. In the circles below name the people you would meet in an average week who are members of these communities.

A family

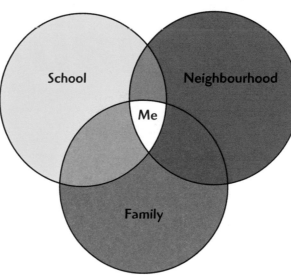

School

Neighbourhood

Me

Family

A school community

2. Are you a member of any other community not mentioned on the signs?

_____

_____

3. What different communities do your family or friends belong to?

_____

_____

_____

_____

4. Do you think it is important for people to take an active part in their community? Explain your answer.

_____

_____

_____

_____

_____

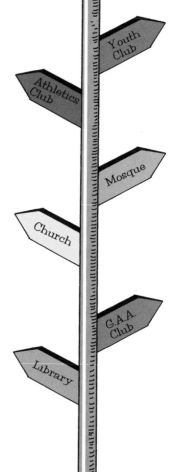

EXERCISE 28 TAKE PART

As a member of many communities you are probably involved in lots of activities. See how much you participate in the communities of which you are a member by completing the following quiz.

1. Do you ...

	Yes	No
a) Get involved in local environmental clean ups?	☐	☐
b) Take part in a local youth club?	☐	☐
c) Take part in the Community Games?	☐	☐
d) Visit the local youth café or No-Name Club?	☐	☐
e) Raise issues with the school's council?	☐	☐
f) Do any volunteer work in your local area?	☐	☐
g) Get involved in local festivals, e.g. the St Patrick's Day parade?	☐	☐
h) Contact your local council over issues that concern you?	☐	☐
i) Campaign for a cause or a local charity, e.g. St Vincent de Paul?	☐	☐
j) Support events or shows in your local area?	☐	☐

2. In what other ways do you participate in the different communities of which you are a member?

   _____

   _____

   _____

   _____

3. What are the benefits of taking part in your local community?

   _____

   _____

   _____

   _____

EXERCISE 29 COUNCILLOR DOGOOD AND DREAMSVILLE

Each local authority is responsible for drawing up a development plan for its area. This is usually done every five years. A development plan normally covers such projects as the development of run-down areas, the improvement of parks and public areas, road improvements, preservation of historical buildings, and what sort of land should be used for housing, schools, factories and shops. After it has been approved by the county councillors, the development plan is put on public display in places like libraries so that any person can make an objection to the plan if they wish.

1. Study this map of a town called Dreamsville and write an email to Councillor Dogood, mentioning:
    a) *any good points*
    b) *any bad points*
    c) *any suggestions you might have to make the proposed new town development better.*

Email to Councillor Dogood

EXERCISE 30 LOCAL COUNCILS

Look at the home page of this county council and answer the questions that follow.

1. What departments are part of Longford County Council?

_____

_____

2. What can you apply for on this site?

_____

_____

3. What can you report on this site?

_____

_____

4. What can you download from this site?

_____

_____

5. What does the 'Latest News' section tell you?

_____

_____

6. In your opinion, what important information about a local area should appear on a county council website?

_____

_____

_____

_____

_____

7. Apart from using websites, how can you find out what is happening in your local area?

_____

_____

_____

8. What is the purpose of Comhairle na nóg?

_____

_____

_____

EXERCISE 31 VOTE FOR ME

Imagine that you are a candidate in a local election. Fill out this election manifesto saying what you will do for your area if you are elected. Keep in mind that local authorities are responsible for certain programmes. Think about what your area needs most.

In your manifesto, say whether you are running as an independent candidate or with a political party.

Hints:

● What about your parks and public areas? Are they in good condition?
● Are there enough recycling depots?
● Do you have a swimming pool?
● What about traffic and parking?
● Are roads in your area in good condition?
● Are there enough places for young people to go, enough things for people to do?
● Do you have an athletics track?
● Do you have a Tidy Towns Committee?
● Should your town be a Fairtrade Town?

Party logo:

Name: _____

Campaign slogan: _____

If I am elected I will

_____

_____

_____

_____

_____

_____

_____

_____

EXERCISE 32 MAKING A STAND

Read the newspaper headlines below and answer the questions that follow.

Residents Take to Streets over Closure of Local Hospital

Environmental Group Take to the Airways over Mobile Phone Masts

Fundraising Campaign to Support Local Sports Complex Launched

Students Twitter over Need for Skate Park

Local Historical group Launch Poster Campaign over Bulldozing of Monument

Local Residents Petition Council over Litter Problem

1. Name six issues that these headlines are highlighting.

   a) _____

   b) _____

   c) _____

   d) _____

   e) _____

   f) _____

2. Name six ways in which these community groups took action over the issues of concern to them.

   a) _____

   b) _____

   c) _____

   d) _____

   e) _____

   f) _____

3. Name one local issue that concerns you and suggest a form of action that you could take over the issue.

   Issue: _____

   _____

   Action: _____

   _____

   _____

   _____

   _____

   _____

   _____

   _____

   _____

EXERCISE 33 LOCAL ACTION

Read the following article and answer the questions that follow.

Group rally over threat to close 500 post offices

Rural rights campaigners protested outside the Dáil yesterday to underline their fury at the threatened closure of more than 500 post office branches nationwide.

The protest – supported by 50 campaigners who travelled to Dublin from all over Cork – warned the coalition that the plight of rural post offices is now set to become a major general election issue.

Campaigners staged a march through Dublin city centre to Kildare St and then held a rally outside the Dáil gates.

The protest aimed to highlight the devastating impact on small communities of the loss of vital services offered by post offices.

Countryside campaigners warned that the loss of more than 500 post offices will cripple many rural communities – and leave some as little more than 'holiday zones' for tourists.

One protester, Tim Ring, warned that the protest march aimed to highlight to the Government and urban dwellers just how dependent country residents are on post offices.

Adapted from an article by Ralph Riegel, *Irish Independent*

1. Over what issue is this group campaigning?

_____

_____

_____

_____

2. What kind of action did this group carry out?

_____

_____

_____

_____

3. What does the protest hope to highlight?

_____

_____

_____

_____

4. In what way do the campaigners believe the loss of post offices will affect their communities?

_____

_____

_____

_____

5. Suggest some other actions that would raise awareness about this issue.

_____

_____

_____

_____

_____

_____

6. In addition to post offices, what other facilities do you think are important to local communities? Explain your choices.

_____

_____

_____

_____

_____

_____

EXERCISE 34 DEVELOPMENT MEANS . . .?

Development in a community may mean different things to different groups, or to different people in a community. Read the statements below about what students think development means in their communities.

Development means that everyone has a TV, DVD player, washing machine and car

Student 1

Development means that everyone can get treated quickly in the local hospital if they are sick

Student 2

Development means having a growing local economy so everyone can get a job and they don't have to go away to somewhere like Australia to get work

Student 3

Development means that young people register to vote so that they can elect people to their local councils who want to bring about change for good

Student 4

Development means we have better transport systems and better roads

Student 5

Development means that everyone has broadband access so you can live and work in your local community

Student 6

Development means people getting involved in local organisations like Tidy Towns to make sure that the environment is kept clean for future generations

Student 7

Development means more parks, playgrounds, sports grounds, and facilities for young people in the community

Student 8

Development means making sure that older people in our community have social services like a community nurse checking up to see if they need anything, and organisations like Meals on Wheels

Student 9

Development means that the local primary school which is in a pre-fab gets replaced with a proper building with modern facilities

Student 10

1. In groups, choose the three statements that most represent development to you. Explain why you have chosen each statement.

   I agree with student _____ **because** _____

   _____

   _____

   _____

   _____

   I agree with student _____ **because** _____

   _____

   _____

   _____

   _____

   I agree with student _____ **because** _____

   _____

   _____

   _____

   _____

2. Add two more ideas about what development means in your local community.

   Idea 1: _____

   _____

   _____

   _____

   Idea 2: _____

   _____

   _____

   _____

3. The founder of the United Nations Human Development Report, Mahbub Ul Haq described human development in the following way:

> Human development is concerned with human dignity: a child who does not die, a disease that does not spread, an ethnic tension that does not explode, a human spirit that is not crushed.

a) How do you think your understanding of development would be different if you were living in a developing country? Explain your answer.

_____

_____

_____

_____

_____

b) How do you think conflict in a community might affect development? Explain your answer.

_____

_____

_____

_____

_____

c) How do you think climate change will affect the development of communities in the future?

_____

_____

_____

_____

_____

EXERCISE 35 DEVELOPMENT FOR WHOM?

Look at the pictures of two different communities in the city of Mumbai in India and answer the questions that follow.

1. Look at the pictures of these two communities in Mumbai and name three ways in which development has, or has not, provided for the needs of the community

   a) _____

   b) _____

   c) _____

2. Looking at the photo of slums in Mumbai, how do you think the conditions could affect the health of its citizens?

   _____

   _____

   _____

   _____

   _____

3. Look back at Exercise 2 and say what rights the citizens in the slums of Mumbai are being denied.

   _____

   _____

   _____

   _____

4. Are you surprised that these two photos were taken in the same city? Explain your answer.

   _____

   _____

   _____

   _____

5. Why do you think development occurs unequally in society?

   _____

   _____

   _____

   _____

EXERCISE 36 ECO DEVELOPMENT

Many developments in communities are aimed at improving the quality of life for citizens. Read the following story about the world's first eco city and answer the questions that follow.

Building cities that are more environmentally friendly

A computer-generated image of Dongtan

In China, there is a lot of interest in planning and building eco cities. Dongtan is the first purpose-built urban area of this kind to be designed and it was planned for Chongming Island, in the Yangtze River delta. The city was designed by a team of urban planning experts at a company called Arup.

The design for the city includes infrastructure that would allow the city's inhabitants to walk to their local bus or tram stop in no more than seven minutes from anywhere in the city. This would reduce the need to drive, and any cars and buses allowed would run on electricity or hydrogen. All citizens would benefit from the many open green spaces, canals and rivers – where water taxis will run.

According to Arup's plan, the city would run mainly on renewable energy – the sun, the wind and biomass. Its waste would be recycled, or used as compost on local farmland to produce food for city residents. The city was designed to use two separate water systems – one for drinking water, and the other for 'grey' water, which would be used for gardens, washing machines, toilets, etc.

Using the same tools and methods, developed when working on Dongtan, eco cities are now being planned across the world.

1. What kind of energy will the planned eco city use? _____

2. Give three ways in which the planned eco city of Dongtan will improve the quality of life for the city's citizens.

a) _____

_____

b) _____

_____

c) _____

_____

3. How will the eco city impact positively on the environment?

_____

_____

_____

4. Do you think this is an example of good development? Give reasons for your answer.

_____

_____

_____

_____

_____

5. Can you think of any ideas that would improve your own area?

_____

_____

_____

_____

6. If you came up with a good idea, who would you contact to discuss it with, and why?

_____

_____

_____

_____

EXERCISE 37 REVISION

Your Community Word Search

Y	A	A	O	B	C	O	S	L	O	N	D	N	S	C
T	W	M	X	I	X	T	Y	A	Z	T	T	N	J	O
I	N	E	I	G	H	B	O	U	R	H	O	O	D	U
R	P	R	O	X	N	J	M	E	U	I	L	Y	M	N
O	K	L	P	Q	J	O	S	T	T	B	B	R	U	C
H	I	T	A	W	A	I	I	C	X	N	G	A	A	I
T	T	R	E	Y	D	J	E	T	N	E	N	R	C	L
U	M	I	G	E	G	L	V	W	I	N	W	B	M	L
A	M	J	N	E	E	R	L	Q	Q	T	A	I	G	O
L	W	T	T	L	G	U	O	K	N	H	E	L	V	R
A	S	O	A	B	N	J	I	U	L	Y	R	P	W	R
C	V	C	Y	B	Y	C	Z	L	N	U	V	F	N	L
O	O	N	G	I	A	P	M	A	C	D	N	J	O	D
L	I	N	P	V	F	J	U	A	K	T	S	D	W	G
D	H	N	E	X	S	R	Z	E	B	I	H	P	V	A

Find these words in the grid above. ◀ ▶ ⊗ ⌂

CAMPAIGN	COUNCILLOR	NEIGHBOURHOOD
LOCAL AUTHORITY	LOCAL ELECTIONS	RESIDENTS
PETITION	PLAYGROUNDS	
VOTE	LIBRARY	

```
                  K  J  M
               I  F  L  Z  T  B  M  P  T
            U  S  V  S  E  M  A  I  L  I  M  Q  V
         Q  Q  S  R  B  F  E  Q  A  K  W  M  X  R  R  M  B
            P  J  F  J  O  O  H  R  B  H  S  T  V  U  E  P  S  S  N
         E  E  C  T  U  O  I  L  S  M  U  W  O  H  S  R  S  E  X  M  N
         Z  X  M  K  H  J  H  P  J  E  F  F  D  W  S  Z  Q  F  Q  U  N
      C  M  K  W  N  N        A  C  A  Q  X        Z  F  U  L  Q  I
      H  L  A  S  N  W        V  V  F  B  O        V  P  D  J  U  W
   P  K  T  F  Q  F  V  M  E  V  L  E  T  T  E  R  V  E  S  R  R  E  E  J
   E  E  E  E  Z  J  X  E  G  N  O  W  D  Z  S  R  E  T  S  O  P  O  S  B  N
   T  X  O  R  P  N  L  P  O  X  B  M  M  A  R  C  H  Q  C  C  H  O  T  Q  S
R  I  S  Y  Y  S  V  O  D  V  L  E  A  F  L  E  T  S  H  F  S  O  I  I  E  Z  T
O  S  S  M  U  H  N  E  M  Q  Y  F  G  E  H  I  E  N  O  E  S  Q  J  O  I  S  L
A  B  T  J  K  W  T  S  K  J  W  L  M  Y  F  U  N  D  R  A  I  S  I  N  G  K  T
   E  I  L  F        I  W  X  Q  U  M  D  L  O  Y  E  V  R  U  S     N  N  C  R
W  B  M  J        A  N  I  H  J  I  C  I  M  Z  C  U  G        B  A  Z  O
B  C  J  P  D        D  H  A  W  R  S  T  N  F  L  M        V  X  I  W  I
   I  C  P  X  N                              S  A  J  R  P
   O  O  P  E  B  O                           A  X  N  U  E  P
      J  C  J  T  F  D  I  A  P  X  Q  W  I  Y  D  W  G  L  C  P  T
      D  A  V  N  I  V  P  G  N  C  P  V  V  W  S  J  Q  W  O  S  G
      G  U  E  S  T  S  P  E  A  K  E  R  Z  A  C  V  V  G  H
         P  N  G  C  I  E  B  C  I  O  K  W  U  X  V  J  I
         A  X  F  O  X  S  R  A  B  C  U  S  U
            J  N  N  G  Z  F  E  O  Y
               T  A  V
```

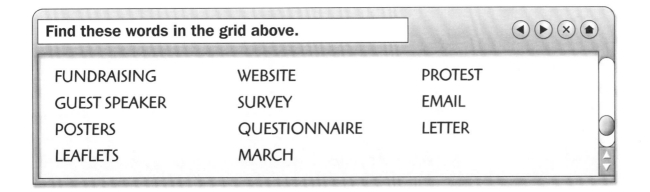

Find these words in the grid above.

◀ ▶ ⊗ ⌂

FUNDRAISING	WEBSITE	PROTEST
GUEST SPEAKER	SURVEY	EMAIL
POSTERS	QUESTIONNAIRE	LETTER
LEAFLETS	MARCH	

Chapter 4

EXERCISE 38 DEMOCRACY AT WORK

The following leaflet describes democracy at work. Read the leaflet and answer the questions that follow.

1. Circle the following words and phrases in the 'Democracy at Work' leaflet.

   ● **Constitution**
   ● **Seanad**
   ● **General Election**
   ● **TDs**
   ● **Laws**
   ● **President**
   ● **Bill**
   ● **Committee**
   ● **Parliamentary**
   ● **Oireachtas**
   ● **Dáil Éireann**
   ● **Democracy**

Ireland's democracy is based on the Constitution. *Achtaíodh an Bunreacht sa bhliain 1937.*

In a general election all Irish people over the age of 18 have a say (a vote) on deciding how they want the country run. *I gcóras daonlathach, is iad an pobal a chinneann cé hiad na daoine ar mian leo iad a bheith i mbun na tíre.*

The Seanad works with the Dáil in the development of the country's laws. *Le bheith ceadaithe sa Dáil agus sa Seanad araon, ní mór tacaíocht níos mó ná a leath (tromlach) de na comhaltaí a bheith le Billí.*

At Dáil Éireann in Leinster House, the TDs elected to represent the people debate new laws (called Bills) and make changes to existing laws. *Sa Dáil, bíonn díospóireacht ag Teachtaí Dála i dtaobh Billí agus féadfaidh siad an Rialtas a cheistiú faoin tslí a bhfuil an tír á rith acu.*

Parliamentary Committees are set up to debate Bills on behalf of the Dáil or the Seanad. This helps to speed up difficult work. *Coistí Oireachtais a dhéanann cuid d'obair na Dála agus an tSeanaid, agus is tábhachtaí ná riamh an chuid sin den obair.*

The President signs a Bill into law when it has been passed by the Dáil and the Seanad. *Nuair a chuireann an tUachtarán a lámh le Bille, is dlí é.*

The Bills passed through the Oireachtas (the President, the Dáil, the Seanad) help make Ireland a safe and fair place for all people to live in. *Is trí na ranna éagsúla rialtais a chuirtear na Billí a ritear san Oireachtas i ngníomh.*

Democracy at work

TITHE AN OIREACHTAIS

HOUSES OF THE OIREACHTAS

2. Choose six of the words you have circled and use each in a sentence to explain what it means.

   a) _____

   b) _____

   c) _____

   d) _____

   e) _____

   f) _____

3. Underline or circle in **red** what age you have to be to vote.
4. Underline or circle in **blue** what TDs do in the Dáil.
5. Underline or circle in **black** what happens at parliamentary committees.
6. Underline or circle in **green** how a bill is signed into law.

EXERCISE 39 GET IT?

Slogans are often used in election campaigns. A slogan is a short phrase that tries to sum up what the candidate or political party believes in. Read the campaign slogans below – these were all used by different candidates in the 2008 American presidential campaign – and answer the questions below.

Yes We Can – Barack Obama

Country First – John McCain

Security. Unity. Prosperity. – Fred Thompson

Tomorrow Begins Today – John Edwards

Hope for America – Ron Paul

Let the People Decide – Mike Gravel

Tested. Ready. Now. – Rudy Giuliani

True Strength for America's Future – Mitt Romney

Solutions for America – Hillary Clinton

Faith. Family. Freedom. – Mike Huckabee

1. What did the candidate Mitt Romney's slogan say that he could provide?

   _____

2. What did the candidate Fred Thompson's slogan say that he could provide?

   _____

3. What did the candidate Hillary Clinton 's slogan say that she could provide?

   _____

4. Which candidate won the 2008 US presidential election?

   _____

5. Do you think that he had a strong campaign slogan? Explain your answer.

   _____

   _____

   _____

6. If you were standing for election to the student council in your school, what campaign slogan would you use?

   _____

   _____

7. Explain how you think the campaign slogan that you have chosen would help you win your campaign.

   _____

   _____

   _____

   _____

   _____

   _____

EXERCISE 40 CAMPAIGN AIDS

Candidates for elections use traditional and new media to help with their political campaigns.

Describe how you think the following forms of communication would be useful in a campaign.

1. a) Twitter: _____

    _____

    b) Blogs: _____

    _____

    c) Facebook/Bebo: _____

    _____

    d) YouTube: _____

    _____

    e) Websites: _____

    _____

    f) Email: _____

    _____

    g) Posters: _____

    _____

    h) Leaflets: _____

    _____

2. Which form of communication do you think would be most effective, and why?

    _____

    _____

    _____

    _____

EXERCISE 41 DOES IT COUNT?

In some countries such as Australia, Italy, Austria, Belgium and Greece, voting is a legal obligation and failure to vote could cost you anything from a fine to 12 months in prison.

Do you think it matters if people vote in elections? Write three arguments for casting your vote and three against.

FOR:

1.	
2.	
3.	

AGAINST:

1.	
2.	
3.	

EXERCISE 42 AT THE TABLE

Look at this cabinet meeting. Can you identify from the list below which minister would say what? Put the most appropriate letter under each number in the table below.

1. Minister for Education and Science
2. Minister for Finance
3. Minister for Communications, Marine and Natural Resources
4. Minister for Community, Rural and Gaeltacht Affairs
5. Minister for Transport
6. Minister for the Environment, Heritage and Local Government
7. Minister for Foreign Affairs
8. Minister for Defence
9. Minister for Agriculture and Food
10. Minister for Justice, Equality and Law Reform
11. Minister for Health and Children
12. Minister for Social and Family Affairs
13. Minister for Enterprise, Trade and Employment
14. Minister for Arts, Sport and Tourism

A. 'I think we should increase unemployment benefit.'
B. 'I want more money for schools.'
C. 'We need to be careful that there isn't another outbreak of foot and mouth.'
D. 'I want to introduce stiffer sentences for joy-riders.'
E. 'I want to expand the Air Corps and Naval Service.'
F. 'I'm concerned about the number of tourists coming to Ireland.'
G. 'I'm hoping to visit some Irish embassies abroad.'
H. 'I want more money to create jobs.'
I. 'I want more laws made to control pollution.'
J. 'What about more support for Irish-speaking areas?'
K. 'I want to introduce higher taxes in the next budget.'
L. 'I want to improve our hospital services.'
M. 'Is anyone here concerned about new EU fishing policies?'
N. 'We need to put more money into the railways.'

1	2	3	4	5	6	7	8	9	10	11	12	13	14
											A		

EXERCISE 43 GOVERNMENT OF IRELAND QUIZ

Circle the correct answers to see how much you know about how Ireland is governed.

1. In Ireland the type of government we have is called:

   Dictatorship   Democracy   Communism

2. Democracy is government of the people:

   By one person   By a king or queen

   By all the people

3. The parliament in Ireland is called:

   Reichstag   Dáil   Senate

4. A person becomes a member of the Dáil by:

   Applying by letter

   Being asked by the president

   Being elected

5. Members of the Dáil are called:

   Ministers   TDs   MEPs

6. The head of the government is called:

   Prime Minister   President   Taoiseach

7. How many TDs sit in the national parliament?

   450   166   70

8. The main job of government is to:

   Run the civil service   Build new transport systems

   Make new laws

9. How many constituencies is Ireland divided into?

   440   42   56

10. Who is the commander-in-chief of the Armed Forces?

    Taoiseach   Tánaiste   President

11. The Seanad is made up of:

   60 senators   45 senators   95 senators

12. The civil service changes when a new government comes in:

   Always   Sometimes   Never

13. The number of ministers in any government is set by the Constitution at no more than:

   5 ministers   40 ministers   15 ministers

14. Which type of government do we have in Ireland now?

   Majority   Minority   Coalition

15. Whose job is it to appoint ministers to a government?

   President   Taoiseach   Civil Service

16. In order to vote in an election you must be aged at least:

   47   18   25

17. A presidential election must be held every:

   4 years   5 years   7 years

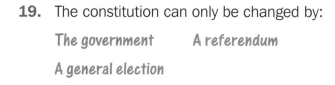

18. A general election must be held every:

   4 years   5 years   7 years

BUNREACHT NA hÉIREANN
CONSTITUTION OF IRELAND

19. The constitution can only be changed by:

   The government   A referendum

   A general election

20. What is the highest court in Ireland?

   Circuit Court   Special Criminal Court

   Supreme Court

My Score: _____
20

EXERCISE 44 **WHAT MATTERS?**

Look at the statements made by these people. What issues do they think are important?

> I think we have to do more about joy-riding.

> I think that we need better transport in our cities.

> I think that we need to do more to protect our environment.

> I think we need to spend more money building up our army and defence forces.

> I think that young people should do more voluntary work.

> I think we should do more for people who are homeless.

> I think we need more jobs for people.

1. Name the seven issues that these people are concerned about.

    a) _____

    b) _____

    c) _____

    d) _____

    e) _____

    f) _____

    g) _____

2. Choose two other issues and say why you think they are of national importance.

    Issue 1: _____

    Why you think it is important: _____

    _____

    _____

    _____

    Issue 2: _____

    Why you think it is important: _____

    _____

    _____

    _____

EXERCISE 45 CHILDREN'S RIGHTS

20 November is Universal Children's Day. Children as a group in society sometimes need special help and protection, and they need people to speak up on their behalf. In Ireland, Barnardos is an organisation that campaigns for children's rights.

Read this campaign page from Barnardos' website and answer the questions that follow.

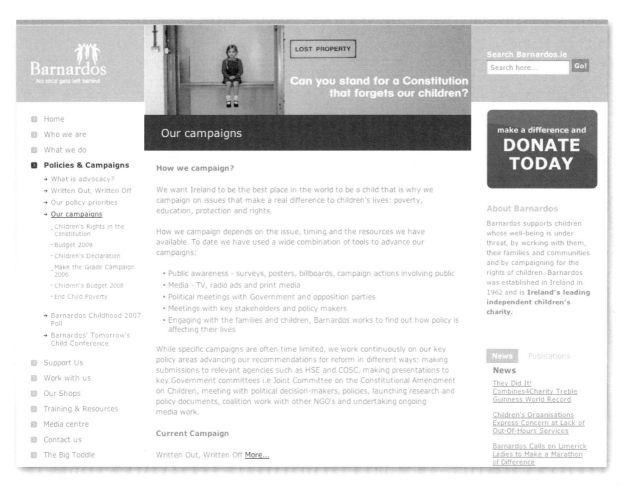

1. What four issues are named that make 'a real difference to children's lives'?

    a) _____

    b) _____

    c) _____

    d) _____

2. Choose **one** issue and suggest three ways in which an improvement in this area would affect children's lives.

    a) _____

    b) _____

    c) _____

3. Name **three** ways in which Barnardos raise awareness about these issues.

   a) _____

   b) _____

   c) _____

4. In what way do you think the media can influence public opinion?

   _____

   _____

   _____

5. What point is the picture at the top of Barnardo's website trying to make?

   _____

   _____

   _____

6. What actions do you think the government could take to improve the lives of children in Ireland?

   _____

   _____

   _____

   _____

7. What is the name of the special payment given by the government to every child in Ireland?

   _____

EXERCISE 46 GET THE PICTURE?

Read the information given on these posters and answer the questions that follow.

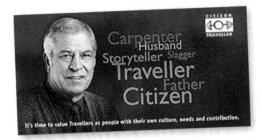

1. What does the poster of the man tell us about him?

_____

_____

_____

2. What does the poster of the child tell us about her?

_____

_____

_____

3. Why do you think so many words are used in each poster?

_____

_____

_____

4. Do you think that this is a good campaign to show that Travellers make a positive contribution to Irish society? Give reasons for your answer.

_____

_____

_____

_____

_____

4

EXERCISE 47 ALONE

ALONE was set up in 1977 by Willie Bermingham and others who were dismayed by the lack of housing and the isolation, loneliness and poverty affecting some older people in our community.

ALONE works with older people, providing long-term housing and combating isolation and loneliness in the community.

ALONE stands for A Little Offering Never Ends.

Read the awareness-raising poster from ALONE and answer the questions that follow.

Older relatives aren't just for Christmas!
They need your company 365 days a year.

Older people living alone are vulnerable to the cold, to illness, to accidents in the home, to loneliness and depression. It only takes five minutes to check on your older neighbour or family member — these five minutes could save their lives, and enrich your own.

PLEASE DON'T LEAVE OLDER PEOPLE **A L O N E**

ALONE, 1 Willie Bermingham Place, Kilmainham Lane, Dublin 8. Tel: 01 6791032. www.alone.ie

1. What point is being made by the headline 'Older relatives aren't just for Christmas'?

   _____

   _____

   _____

2. How are some older persons 'vulnerable'?

   _____

   _____

   _____

3. What action does the poster suggest you can take when you see a vulnerable person?

   _____

   _____

   _____

4. How can the government help to look out for the rights of older people?

   _____

   _____

   _____

EXERCISE 48 INFLUENCE IT!

Imagine that you work for an advertising agency. You have been hired by a group in Irish society that does not feel they have been treated equally. The group wants you to produce a poster.

This group wants to have a positive image to use in their campaign to show why they should be treated equally. They want the campaign to show that they make a positive contribution to Irish society. They do not want to be pitied by anyone.

Name the group that you are working for and design your poster in the billboard below.

Name of group: _____

(Exercise adapted from *All Different All Equal*, National Youth Council of Ireland.)

EXERCISE 49 BUILDING YOUR CAMPAIGN

Raising awareness on an issue that concerns you might involve carrying out a campaign to gather support and influence people's opinion. Written on the bricks below are some of the ways a campaign can be helped or hindered.

1. Use **green** to colour the bricks that would help you in your campaign.

2. Use **red** to colour the bricks that would not help your campaign.

3. **Choose** five ways in which a campaign can be made successful. Rank them in order of importance.

a) _____

b) _____

c) _____

d) _____

e) _____

4. Name one other way in which a campaign could be helped and one other way in which it could be hindered.

Helped: _____

_____

Hindered: _____

_____

5. Name some personal skills that you can develop by taking part in campaigns on issues that concern you.

_____

_____

_____

_____

EXERCISE 50 YOUR CONSTITUTION

The Constitution of Ireland (Bunreacht na hÉireann) contains the basic laws of our country. It describes the powers of the president and the government, and protects the rights of citizens. It states that every citizen has the right to, for example:

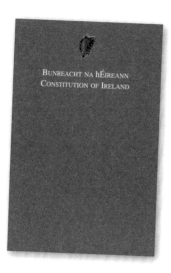

practise their religion; education; vote; own and inherit property; freedom and equal treatment under the law.

Read the following passage from the Constitution and answer the questions that follow.*

'The State guarantees in its laws to respect, and as far as possible, by its laws to defend . . . the personal rights of the citizen.

'The State shall, in particular, by its laws protect . . . the life, person, good name, and property rights of every citizen . . .

'The State guarantees liberty for the exercise of the following rights:

. . . the right of the citizens to express freely their convictions and opinions

. . . the right of the citizens to assemble peaceably and without arms

. . . the right of the citizens to form associations and unions.'

* Adapted from Junior Cert CSPE exam paper, 2002.

1. Name **three** rights that are mentioned on the previous page. For each right, give one reason why it is important.

   a) _____

   Reason: _____

   _____

   _____

   b) _____

   Reason: _____

   _____

   _____

   c) _____

   Reason: _____

   _____

   _____

2. The right of citizens 'to express freely their convictions and opinions' is mentioned. Explain what this means. Do you consider it an important right?

   _____

   _____

   _____

   _____

3. The Constitution of Ireland can only be changed by a referendum. What is a referendum? Can you name any issues over which we have had a referendum?

   A referendum is _____

   _____

   _____

   Issues: _____

   _____

   _____

   _____

EXERCISE 51 EQUALITY AND THE LAW

Under the Employment Equality Acts (1998 and 2004) and the Equal Status Acts (2000 and 2004) you cannot discriminate against a person on the following grounds:

- race
- gender
- disability
- religion
- family status

- marital status
- being a member of the Travelling community
- sexual orientation
- age.

1. In the space below each picture, say on what grounds the person is being discriminated against. (*Hint:* Look at the list above.)

a) This person is being discriminated against on the grounds of

_____.

b) This person is being discriminated against on the grounds of

_____.

c) This person is being discriminated against on the grounds of

_____.

d) This person is being discriminated against on the grounds of

_____.

2. Fill in the blanks:

__ __ S __ __ __ __ __ __ __ __ __ __ __ means treating someone less favourably than you would treat another person. In the above cases, you would be breaking the

__ A __.

EXERCISE 52 CRIME STOP

Crimestoppers is an organisation that works with the Gardaí and the community to help solve crime. Study the poster and answer the questions about it.

1. What **three** points have Crimestoppers put on their poster to encourage people to phone them?

   a) _____

   b) _____

   c) _____

2. Name **two** business companies or organisations that are supporting this campaign.

   a) _____

   b) _____

3. Many crimes commited in Ireland are related to drug abuse. Can you explain the connection?

_____

_____

_____

4. Describe **two** actions that a local community could take to try and stop crime in their area. These actions must not break the law.

a) _____

_____

_____

b) _____

_____

_____

5. Suggest **two** reasons why it might be difficult for a young person to report a crime.

a) _____

_____

_____

b) _____

_____

_____

(Adapted from the Junior Certificate examination 2000, Department of Education and Science.)

EXERCISE 53 REVISION

Voting Word Search

Z	L	H	B	K	D	F	D	Y	H	R	H	D	E	R
N	O	I	T	A	T	S	G	N	I	L	L	O	P	E
B	C	F	Q	O	O	F	H	M	Y	I	P	O	T	P
Q	V	H	L	B	O	U	Z	C	Z	N	L	N	Q	A
L	T	X	R	O	R	B	A	O	V	I	A	V	H	P
K	W	J	T	V	D	R	G	F	U	L	K	G	B	T
L	C	F	E	J	C	S	L	N	P	E	K	H	U	O
E	S	P	U	O	F	C	M	V	I	H	M	I	G	L
E	L	P	M	C	W	V	J	U	F	L	W	D	E	L
L	I	E	X	Y	C	R	A	W	K	O	L	B	I	A
Q	D	W	C	A	O	D	S	W	K	S	X	O	E	B
U	A	D	V	T	W	A	K	K	C	K	D	E	P	P
O	B	Z	F	V	I	Z	W	D	V	X	C	Q	H	B
T	L	O	P	Z	I	O	R	E	G	I	S	T	E	R
A	A	M	B	E	M	B	N	P	I	G	K	R	R	N

Find these words in the grid above.

◄ ► ⊗ ⌂

BALLOT PAPER	POLLING BOOTH	REGISTER
DEMOCRACY	POLLING STATION	
ELECTION	QUOTA	

Election Steps Reorder

These are the steps in voting in an election. They are mixed up. Put them in the right order by using the table below.

A. Bring your polling card.

B. Put your name on the Register of Electors.

C. Go to the polling station.

D. Fill in your ballot paper.

E. Go to a polling booth.

1.	Put your name on the Register of Electors.
2.	
3.	
4.	
5.	

Check out your *Impact!* textbook to see if you've got it right!

Government Word Search

N	B	T	N	G	Q	A	V	E	H	S	E	Q	U	D
P	O	I	H	Z	B	U	D	C	B	T	S	K	G	K
N	K	I	D	E	J	F	A	B	O	H	U	K	J	R
M	L	D	T	K	S	E	Q	D	R	E	O	U	L	A
G	R	M	H	C	S	E	U	I	X	D	H	C	K	W
M	B	Q	W	I	E	M	A	D	H	A	R	I	C	O
I	Q	B	O	B	B	L	F	N	J	I	E	K	P	Y
J	G	A	R	C	E	C	E	J	A	L	T	P	G	N
N	T	D	R	C	N	M	F	L	W	D	S	R	B	M
G	Z	Y	L	W	V	Q	V	K	A	N	N	B	A	T
R	S	U	O	D	A	Z	U	J	V	R	I	H	U	Q
I	M	I	N	I	S	T	E	R	S	L	E	A	J	X
W	A	L	V	T	V	K	P	S	L	D	L	N	S	X
G	N	B	V	Z	E	R	J	S	J	G	J	Z	E	R
Z	I	Y	R	N	D	E	E	U	G	F	A	O	L	G

Find these words in the grid above.

BILLS	LEINSTER HOUSE	THE DAIL
GENERAL ELECTION	MINISTERS	THE SEANAD
LAW	TAOISEACH	

Word Grid

Use these clues to complete the word grid.

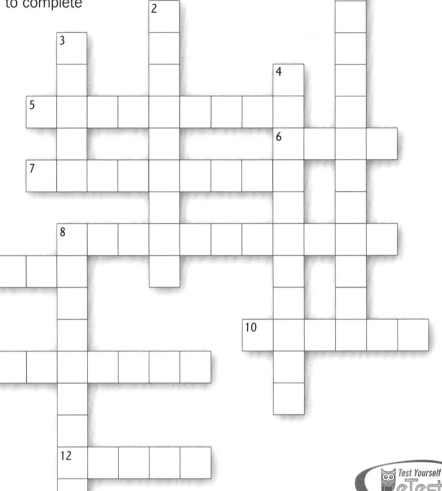

Across

5. This is a government that is made up of two or more parties.
6. 166 TDs meet here.
7. What you are called if you stand for election.
8. Ministers are in charge of these.
9. Everyone over 18 has the right to do this.
10. One of the houses of the Oireachtas.
11. You go out and vote in one of these.
12. The sorting of votes happens at a _____.

Down

1. This contains the basic laws of our country.
2. A kind of party you could join.
3. A person needs to reach this before they can be elected.
4. A person who is not a member of a political party.
8. Government of the people by the people.

Chapter 5

EXERCISE 54 THE EU

Below is a map of the 27 countries of the EU.

1. On the map, write in the countries' capitals that are missing.

2. Which country in the centre of Europe is not a member of the EU?

3. Which Scandinavian country is not a member of the EU?

4. Which **three** European countries are likely to become members of the EU?

   a) _____

   b) _____

   c) _____

5. Here are the profiles of 12 of the countries that have joined the EU since 2004. Fill in the name of the country on each flag below.

Latvia   Lithuania   Hungary   Romania

Estonia   Slovenia   Czech Republic   Bulgaria

Slovakia   Cyprus   Malta   Poland

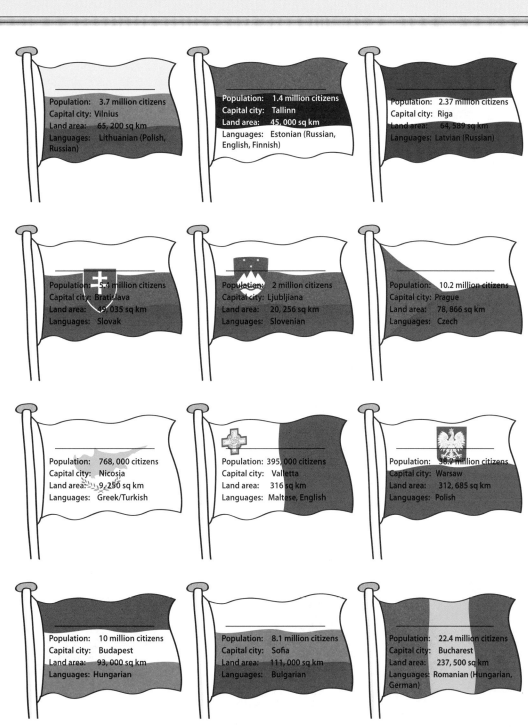

Population: 3.7 million citizens
Capital city: Vilnius
Land area: 65, 200 sq km
Languages: Lithuanian (Polish, Russian)

Population: 1.4 million citizens
Capital city: Tallinn
Land area: 45, 000 sq km
Languages: Estonian (Russian, English, Finnish)

Population: 2.37 million citizens
Capital city: Riga
Land area: 64, 589 sq km
Languages: Latvian (Russian)

Population: 5.4 million citizens
Capital city: Bratislava
Land area: 49, 035 sq km
Languages: Slovak

Population: 2 million citizens
Capital city: Ljubljiana
Land area: 20, 256 sq km
Languages: Slovenian

Population: 10.2 million citizens
Capital city: Prague
Land area: 78, 866 sq km
Languages: Czech

Population: 768, 000 citizens
Capital city: Nicosia
Land area: 9, 250 sq km
Languages: Greek/Turkish

Population: 395, 000 citizens
Capital city: Valletta
Land area: 316 sq km
Languages: Maltese, English

Population: 38.7 million citizens
Capital city: Warsaw
Land area: 312, 685 sq km
Languages: Polish

Population: 10 million citizens
Capital city: Budapest
Land area: 93, 000 sq km
Languages: Hungarian

Population: 8.1 million citizens
Capital city: Sofia
Land area: 111, 000 sq km
Languages: Bulgarian

Population: 22.4 million citizens
Capital city: Bucharest
Land area: 237, 500 sq km
Languages: Romanian (Hungarian, German)

EXERCISE 55 EURO QUIZ

Some of the answers to this quiz can be found in the last exercise.

DEUTSCHLAND
EUROPA
Berlin: Brandenburger Tor

EUROPA
PORTUGAL
Lisboa: A Torre de Belém

NEDERLAND
EUROPA
Amsterdam: Kanaal en typische huizen

DANMARK
EUROPA
København: Den Lille Havirue

FINLAND
EUROPA
Helsihgfors : Sibelius-monumentti

LUXEMBOURG
EUROPA
Pont Adolphe

ELLAS
EUROPA
Αθήνα: Παρθενώνας

ÖSTERREICH
EUROPA
Wien: Stephansdom

ESPAÑA
EUROPA
Madrid: Palacio Real

IRELAND
EUROPA
Dublin: The Four Courts

BELGIE - BELGIQUE
EUROPA
Manneken-pis
Brussel - Bruxelles

EUROPA
UNITED KINGDOM
London: Big Ben

EUROPA
FRANCE
Paris: la Tour Eiffel

SVERIGE
EUROPA
Stokholms Stadhus

EUROPA
ITALIA
Roma: Il Colosseo

1. In which country would you dance the flamenco?

    _____

2. In which country would you visit the Acropolis?

    _____

3. In which country would you be if you found yourself in the city of Bucharest?

    _____

4. In which country would you visit the Child of Prague?

    _____

5. In which country would you eat a baguette or go to see the Mona Lisa?

    _____

6. In which country would you be if you found yourself in the city of Bratislava?

    _____

7. In which country would you eat sauerkraut and sausage?

    _____

8. In which country would you be if you were in the city of Riga?

    _____

9. In which country would you be if you took a stroll in the largest park in Europe?

    _____

10. In which country would you be if you found yourself in the city of Tallinn?

    _____

11. In which country would you be if you crossed from Denmark and got off the train in Malmö?

    _____

12. In which country would you be if you found yourself in the city of Ljubljana?

    _____

13. In which country would you be if you found yourself in front of the European Court of Justice?

    _____

14. In which country would you see Big Ben?

    _____

15. In which country would you be if you found yourself in the city of Warsaw?

_____

16. Which country might remind you of Mozart and ski resorts?

_____

17. On which island country would you be if you found yourself in the city of Nicosia?

_____

18. In which country would you travel along canals in the capital and visit tulip farms?

_____

19. On which island country would you be if you found yourself in the city of Valletta?

_____

20. In which country would you see the famous statue of the Little Mermaid?

_____

21. In which country could you travel by gondola under the Bridge of Sighs?

_____

22. In which country would you be if you found yourself in the city of Sofia?

_____

23. In which country could you eat delicious handmade chocolate?

_____

24. In which country would you find the manufacturer of Nokia mobile phones?

_____

25. In which country would you find a sun-soaked coastline called the Algarve?

_____

26. In which country would you be if you found yourself in the city of Budapest?

_____

27. In which country would you be if you found yourself in the city of Vilnius?

_____

Total score: _____
                27

EXERCISE 56 WHO DOES WHAT IN THE EU?

Match the name of each European institutions with the correct description of the work it does by putting the correct letters in the table below.

A Suggests/proposes new laws and makes sure any agreements are carried out.

B Has the final say on what becomes EU law.

C Has the power to request a member state to change any law that is not in keeping with EU law and can fine any member state that fails to do so.

D Makes sure that the EU budget is properly spent.

E Debates the suggestions and proposals for new laws in Strasbourg.

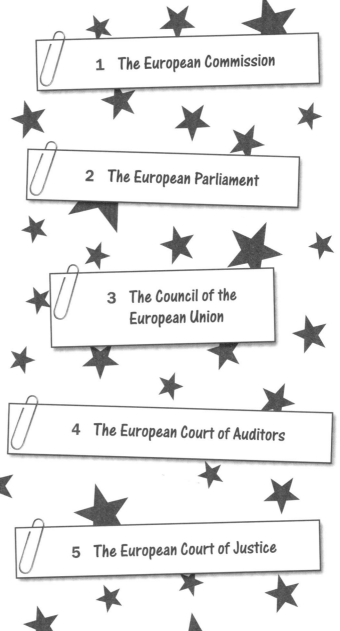

1 The European Commission

2 The European Parliament

3 The Council of the European Union

4 The European Court of Auditors

5 The European Court of Justice

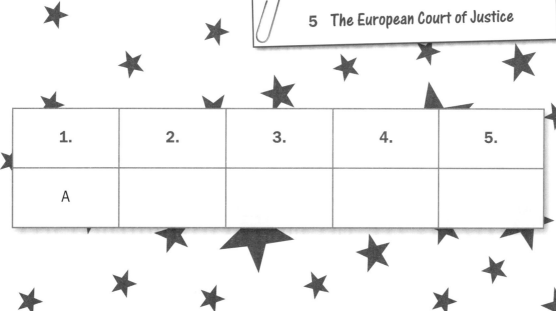

1.	2.	3.	4.	5.
A				

EXERCISE 57 VOTE FOR YOUR MEP

The ballot paper below is from the 2009 European Parliament election and shows the candidates for Dublin. Examine the ballot paper and answer the questions that follow.

Toghchán do Pharlaimint na hEorpa
European Parliament Election

TREORACHA

1. Scríobh an figiúr 1 sa bhosca le hais ghrianghraf an chéad iarrthóra is rogha leat, scríobh an figiúr 2 sa bhosca le hais ghrianghraf an iarrthóra do dhara rogha, agus mar sin de.
2. Fill an páipéar ionas nach bhfeicfear do vóta. Taispeáin *cúl an pháipéir* don oifigeach ceannais, agus cuir sa bhosca ballóide e.

INSTRUCTIONS

1. Write 1 in the box beside the photograph of the candidate of your first choice, write 2 in the box beside the photograph of the candidate of your second choice, and so on.
2. Fold the paper to conceal your vote. Show the *back of the paper* to the presiding officer and put it in the ballot box.

BYRNE – FIANNA FÁIL
(EIBHLIN BYRNE of Mansion House, Dawson Street, Dublin 2; Lord Mayor of Dublin)
Liosta Ionaid FF Replacement List

De BÚRCA – GREEN PARTY/ COMHAONTAS GLAS
(DÉIRDRE De BÚRCA of 11 Highland Grove, The Park, Cabinteely, Co Dublin; Public Representative (Senator))
Liosta Ionaid GP/CG Replacement List

De ROSSA – THE LABOUR PARTY
(PROINSIAS De ROSSA of 14ᵗʰ Floor, Liberty Hall, Dublin 1; M.E.P.)
Liosta Ionaid LP Replacement List

HIGGINS – THE SOCIALIST PARTY
(JOE HIGGINS of 155 Briarwood Close, Dublin 15; Political Activist)
Liosta Ionaid SP Replacement List

McDONALD – SINN FÉIN
(MARY LOU McDONALD of 23 Ashington Heath, Navan Road, Dublin 7; Public Representative)
Liosta Ionaid SF Replacement List

McKENNA – NON PARTY
(PATRICIA McKENNA of 11 Iona Road, Glasnevin, Dublin 9; Public Activist)
Liosta Ionaid PMcK Replacement List

MITCHELL – FINE GAEL
(GAY MITCHELL of 192 Upper Rathmines Road, Dublin 6; MEP)
Liosta Ionaid FG Replacement List

RYAN – FIANNA FÁIL
(EOIN RYAN of Sussex Rd, Dublin 4; MEP)
Liosta Ionaid FF Replacement List

SIMONS – LIBERTAS
(CAROLINE SIMONS of Denshaw House, Baggot Street, Dublin 2)

SWEENEY – NON PARTY
(EMMANUEL SWEENEY of 23, Ormond Road, Ranelagh, Dublin 6, Ireland; Writer)
Liosta Ionaid ES Replacement List

1. How do you mark the ballot paper showing your first, second, third, etc. choice of candidate?

   _____

   _____

   _____

   _____

2. What political parties are represented on this ballot paper?

   _____

   _____

   _____

   _____

   _____

3. How many candidates describe themselves as 'Non Party'? _____

4. Which **three** candidates were elected for the Dublin area in the 2009 European Parliament elections?

   a) _____

   b) _____

   c) _____

5. How long is the term of office of an MEP? _____

EXERCISE 58 EUROPE DAY

The European Union chose 9 May as the date to celebrate 'Europe Day'.
Imagine your school has decided to highlight Europe Day.

1. Name **three** activities you would organise in the school on Europe Day.

    a) _____

    b) _____

    c) _____

2. Write a speech that you would give at a school assembly on the day. You could
   include information on why the EU was set up and some important changes that
   have happened since Ireland joined the EU.

   _____

   _____

   _____

   _____

   _____

   _____

   _____

   _____

   _____

   _____

   _____

   _____

   _____

   _____

   _____

   _____

   _____

   _____

INTERDEPENDENCE

5

INTERDEPENDENCE

3. Design a poster and slogan that could be put up in the school to highlight Europe Day.

United in diversity

9 May – Europe Day

European Union

102

EXERCISE 59 THE UNITED NATIONS DEVELOPMENT REPORT

This is the UN logo. The world is cradled by two olive branches, suggesting peace.

The United Nations produces facts and figures about how the world is developing and which parts of the world are suffering from a lack of development. The United Nations Human Development Index, which is published every year by the United Nations Development Programme (UNDP, one of many UN agencies), includes information on countries, such as life expectancy at birth, numbers of boys and girls in education, population growth, average income per person, the number of doctors per thousand people, how many people have access to the Internet, etc.

Look at the figures on life expectancy from a recent UN Development Report and answer the questions below.

The five countries with the highest life expectancy:

Country	Years
1 Japan	82.2
2 Hong Kong, China	81.8
3 Iceland	80.9
4 Switzerland	80.7
5 Australia	80.5

The five countries with the lowest life expectancy:

Country	Years
1 Swaziland	31.3
2 Botswana	34.9
3 Lesotho	35.2
4 Zimbabwe	36.6
5 Zambia	37.7

1. In what country could you expect to live longest? _____

2. In what country would your expected life span be shortest? _____

3. Give **three** possible reasons that might account for such short life expectancy in the African countries listed.

   Reason 1: _____

   _____

   _____

   Reason 2: _____

   _____

   _____

   Reason 3: _____

   _____

   _____

4. Think of **two** actions that could be taken to improve life expectancy in the African countries listed.

   Action 1: _____

   _____

   _____

   Action 2: _____

   _____

   _____

5. How could your class make this issue the basis of an action project?

   _____

   _____

   _____

   _____

EXERCISE 60 UNITED NATIONS AGENCIES

The United Nations has a number of special agencies that try to help find solutions to global problems.

1. Match the logo to the correct UN organisation/agency by drawing a connecting line. The first one has been done for you.

United Nations Development Programme

United Nations High Commissioner for Refugees

United Nations Children's Fund

United Nations International Research and Training Institute for the Advancement of Women

Food and Agriculture Organisation of the United Nations

2. Redesign the logo of UNEP (United Nations Environment Programme) below.

Existing logo

Your logo

EXERCISE 61 DEVELOPMENT GOALS

In 2000, 189 members of the United Nations signed the Millennium Development Goals. These goals are about ending world poverty, and targets have been set for 2015.

1. Match the Millennium Development Goals with the facts in the grid opposite.

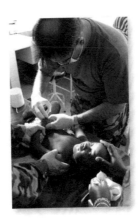

Goals

Goal 1	Reduce poverty.
Goal 2	Educate every child.
Goal 3	Provide equal chances for girls and women.
Goal 4	Reduce the numbers of babies and children who die.
Goal 5	Ensure a safe and healthy motherhood.
Goal 6	Fight diseases like HIV/Aids and malaria.
Goal 7	Clean up the environment.
Goal 8	Share responsibility for making the world a better place.

Facts

Fact A	In 2000, every 14 seconds another child became an orphan due to an Aids-related death.
Fact B	If rich countries made trade fairer, poor countries could earn up to $700 billion a year.
Fact C	64 per cent of the world's adults who cannot read and write are women.
Fact D	1.2 billion people live on less than $1 a day.
Fact E	115 million children of primary school age are not in school.
Fact F	Every year more than 5 million women die as a result of pregnancy and childbirth.
Fact G	Every year more than 10 million babies and children die, many from preventable diseases.
Fact H	1 in 5 children in the developing world do not have clean water.

Goal 1	Goal 2	Goal 3	Goal 4	Goal 5	Goal 6	Goal 7	Goal 8
Fact:	Fact:	Fact:	Fact:	Fact:	Fact:	Fact:	Fact:

Adapted from 'Chinya', a CSPE resource produced by Trócaire.

2. Which **three** UN Development Goals would you try and find solutions to? Give a reason for each of your choices.

   a) Goal: _____

   Reason for choice: _____

   _____

   b) Goal: _____

   Reason for choice: _____

   _____

   c) Goal: _____

   Reason for choice: _____

   _____

EXERCISE 62 UNITED NATIONS QUIZ

A meeting of the UN Security council

United Nations headquarters

1. What is the UN General Assembly?

   _____

2. Who is the UN General Secretary?

   _____

3. What is the main aim of the Security Council?

   _____

   _____

   _____

4. How many members does the UN Security Council have? _____

5. Name one of the permanent members of the Security Council. _____

6. Where are the UN headquarters? _____

7. What is the full name of the UN organisation UNHCR?

   _____

   _____

   _____

8. Who wears blue helmets with a UN crest on them?

_____

_____

_____

9. 10 December is United Nations _____ _____ Day.

10. Can you name a famous Irish person who has held a major job in the United Nations?

_____

11. How many member states are there in the United Nations? _____

12. Name a famous UN Goodwill Ambassador. _____

13. Name a country where members of the Irish defence forces have served as part of a UN peacekeeping mission.

_____

14. What does the power of veto on the UN Security Council mean?

_____

_____

_____

15. What is the name of the UN website that was specially designed for school students?

_____

(See your *Impact!* textbook to help you with the quiz.)

Total score: _____
15

◀ ▶ ⊗ ⌂

EXERCISE 63 PEOPLE ON THE MOVE

There are many different reasons why people move around the world. Sometimes they are fleeing from war and persecution, sometimes they are looking for a better way of life. Read the following profiles of Himpka, Sam, Mohammed, Matthew and Michelle.

Profiles

1 As a result of war in Kosovo, Himpka was invited by the Irish government to come and live in Ireland.

2 When the factory Sam worked in closed down in Limerick he saw lots of advertisements in the paper for jobs in New York. He decided to move there in search of better job opportunities.

3 When fighting broke out in Kabul, Mohammed was forced to leave his home in the capital of Afghanistan and hide in the mountains of the north.

4 When the rebels got near their village, Matthew and his mother fled Sierra Leone. They stowed away on a ship going to France. Matthew's uncle, who was already in France, took them in.

5 Michelle left Algeria because of religious persecution. When she reached Ireland she went straight to the Department of Justice and stated that she wished to apply to live in Ireland.

Descriptions

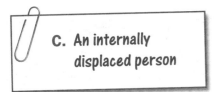

C. An internally
displaced person

A. An economic migrant

B. A programme refugee

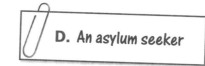

D. An asylum seeker

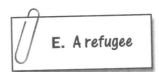

E. A refugee

1. Match each person with the correct profile, A–E.

Himpka	B
Sam	
Mohammed	
Matthew	
Michelle	

2. Why did Michelle, Sam and Mohammed leave their homes?

   a) Michelle: _____

   _____

   b) Sam: _____

   _____

   c) Mohammed: _____

   _____

3. Give two other reasons why people might be forced to leave their own homes.

   a) _____

   _____

   b) _____

   _____

EXERCISE 64 HOW DOES IT FEEL?

The United Nations has a number of special agencies that try to solve world problems. One of these agencies is the United Nations High Commission for Refugees. Part of the work that it does is to highlight the difficulties faced by refugees around the world.

Read the message on this poster and answer the questions below.

1. According to the poster, how do people become refugees?

   _____

   _____

   _____

2. Why, according to the poster, do refugees need help?

   _____

   _____

   _____

HOW DOES IT FEEL?

Imagine this.
   You've lived all your life at peace. Home, family, friends, all normal. Then, without warning, your whole world changes.
   Overnight, lifelong neighbours become lifelong enemies. Tanks prowl the streets and buses burn. Mortar shells shatter the mosques. Rockets silence the church bells.
   Suddenly everything you've known and owned and loved is gone and, if you're lucky enough to survive, you find yourself alone and bewildered in a foreign land. You are a refugee.

How does it feel?
   The fact is, refugees are just like you and me, except that they have nothing. And that's exactly what they'll always have unless we help.
   We're not asking for money (though every contribution helps), but only this:
   When you do meet a refugee, imagine

UNHCR

data courtesy of the LEGO Group.

United Nations High Commissioner for Refugees

for a moment what it must be like, an then show her your smile. Instead of y back.
   It may not seem much. But to a refugee it can mean everything.
   UNHCR is a strictly humanitarian organization funded only by voluntary contributions. Currently it is responsi for more than 27 million refugees aro the world.

UNHCR Public Information
P.O. Box 2500
1211 Geneva 2, Switzerland

3. What does this poster say you should do when you meet a refugee?

   _____

   _____

4. What organisation produced this poster? _____

5. Do you think that this poster works well to raise awareness about refugees? Explain your answer.

   _____

   _____

6. Can you name any other organisations that help refugees?

   _____

   _____

EXERCISE 65 DOES YOUR WIFE WORK?

Read this story and answer the questions that follow.

'Have you many children?' the doctor asked.

'God has not been good to me. Of sixteen born, only nine live,' he answered.

'Does your wife work?'

'No, she stays at home.'

'I see. How does she spend her day?'

'Well, she gets up in the morning, fetches water and wood, makes the fire and cooks breakfast. Then she goes down to the river and washes clothes. After that she goes to town to get corn ground and buys what we need in the market. Then she cooks the midday meal.'

'You come home at midday?'

'No, no. She brings the meal to me in the fields – about three kilometres from home.'

'And after that?'

'Well, she takes care of the hens and pigs. And of course she looks after the children all day. Then she prepares supper so that it is ready when I come home.'

'Does she go to bed after supper?'

'No, I do. She has things to do around the house until nine o'clock.'

'But you say your wife doesn't work?'

'No, I told you. She stays at home.'

Source: International Labour Organisation

1. Name six jobs this woman does.

   a) _____   d) _____

   b) _____   e) _____

   c) _____   f) _____

2. Why does her husband say she doesn't work, do you think?

   _____

   _____

3. Suggest a way in which the world could change so that women could achieve equality.

   _____

   _____

EXERCISE 66 THE RED CROSS FAMILY

Read the information below about the Red Cross and answer the questions that follow.

Irish Red Cross volunteers give their time freely every day in your local community, and practise their first aid skills in events throughout the year to maintain their high standards. Here, Irish Red Cross members Ryan Mulholland, Mary Lynch and Orla Sheridan are pictured putting their skills to the test at a first aid competition by treating Peadar Middleton after a simulated cycling accident.

In the aftermath of any disaster, clean water and supplies are essential to survivors. In Myanmar (Burma), after cyclone Nargis struck, people lined banks and jetties and waded out to Red Cross boats to get supplies.

Restoring family links in the Democratic Republic of the Congo. Seven former soldiers are joyfully reunited with their families.

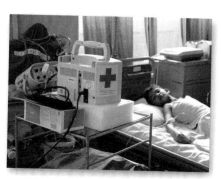

The Red Cross was set up by a young Swiss citizen, Henri Dunant, after he witnessed a battle between Austrian and French troops in 1859 that left 36,000 men dead or wounded on the battlefield. He set up a field hospital in a church, and he got helpers to dress wounds, carry water and write farewell letters to the families of dying men. He noticed that all the helpers forgot about the nationality of the men they helped. They were all brothers now.

The famous symbol of the Red Cross is the Swiss national flag inverted.

Source: adapted from *Exploring Humanitarian Law*,
International Committee of the Red Cross

1. Explain in your own words how the Red Cross was started.

_____

_____

_____

The Red Cross Family

National societies like the Irish Red Cross run programmes in health such as first aid, community care, youth work and emergency programmes to help the local population.

The International Federation of Red Cross and Red Crescent societies organises international relief operations when natural disasters occur.

The International Committee of the Red Cross provides protection and help to victims of armed conflict, without taking sides.

For more information on how you can get involved with the Irish Red Cross, check on www.redcross.ie or check them out on Facebook.

2. Describe some of the work done by the Red Cross Family.

_____

_____

_____

The Red Cross Tracing Service

The Red Cross also has a tracing service to reunite families. In the chaos of armed conflict, families can be forced to flee their homes and family members are often separated. More than half of the estimated fifty million refugees and internally displaced people in the world are children and teenagers. More than two million are children who have been separated from their families. As children without parents or carers, they are often subject to abuse and recruitment as child soldiers.

3. What sometimes happens to children in war situations when they have no parents or carers?

_____

_____

_____

EXERCISE 67 KNOW RACISM

Racism is based on the false belief that some 'peoples' are superior to others. It is a form of discrimination faced by ethnic minority groups* that denies people basic human rights, dignity and respect.

This is a poster designed by students to raise awareness on the issue of racism.

1. What point is being made by the image in the poster?

2. Design your own version of the poster.

3. This is the symbol of the Irish government's anti-racism campaign. The emblem's message is 'Five Continents – One People'. It was designed by John Rocha.

*An ethnic minority group is a group of people whose skin colour, religion or culture is different from the majority of people living in the same place.

Design your own anti-racist badge in the space below.

EXERCISE 68 THE RICHNESS OF DIVERSITY

There are people of 160 different nationalities now living in Ireland. Each nationality has its own culture and traditions.

1. Think about all the different ways in which different cultures have added to our lives in Ireland, and say where these influences have come from. Look at the pictures to help you with your answers.

Influence	Culture/Country
Music	
_____	_____
_____	_____
Food	
_____	_____
_____	_____
Clothes	
_____	_____
_____	_____
Media/TV	
_____	_____
_____	_____
Leisure/Sports	
_____	_____
_____	_____

2. Can you add any other countries and describe how they have influenced our lives?

    _____

    _____

    _____

    _____

(Adapted from *A Young Person's Guide to Cultural Diversity in Northern Ireland*)

EXERCISE 69 FAIR PLAY TO YOU!

Fairtrade is one way in which you can help people in the developing world. Study the poster below and answer the questions that follow.

1. What items featured on this poster may carry the Fairtrade logo?

    _____

    _____

2. In what ways does Sarah from Uganda believe that buying goods with the Fairtrade logo will be of benefit?

    _____

    _____

3. Can you name any other goods in Irish shops or cafés that carry the Fairtrade mark?

    _____

    _____

    _____

4. What actions could you take at home and at school to support the Fairtrade campaign?

    _____

    _____

    _____

EXERCISE 70 CHILD LABOUR

Forced labour and slave labour are not a thing of the past. They exist today in many parts of the world and can take different forms. Many children are forced to work as slave labourers in agriculture and domestic service while others are recruited against their will as child soldiers.

Read the story below and answer the questions that follow.

A girl child sold into slavery in Sudan

'My wife and four children were abducted during a raid . . . Three of my children and my wife managed to escape, but my eight-year-old daughter remained behind. She is now kept by a man who bought her from her captor. When I discovered where she was, I went north and tried to get her back by legal means. I opened a case against the man at the police station, and had to pay the police 20,000 Sudanese pounds [approximately US$250] to do this.

'A police officer accompanied me to the home of the man. This man refused to give me my girl and demanded 50,000 Sudanese pounds for her release. The policeman said that as the man had bought the girl from her captor, she was his property and he could not insist on her release.

'I was forced to leave her there where she is badly mistreated by the man's wife. I also lost the 20,000 pounds which the policeman refused to return to me. I had to return home empty-handed.'

Source: Nelien Haspels and Michele Jankanish: *Action Against Child Labour*, International Labour Office (2000)

---

1. Why was the man unable to get his daughter back?

    _____

    _____

    _____

2. What kind of work do you think the child is being used for?

    _____

    _____

    _____

3. What does this story tell you about how children are valued?

_____

_____

_____

4. Name three rights this child is being denied.

a) _____

b) _____

c) _____

5. In your opinion, what actions could be taken to end child labour?

Action 1: _____

_____

Action 2: _____

_____

6. In your opinion, what is the connection between not going to school as a child because you have to work, and staying in poverty as an adult?

_____

_____

_____

_____

7. What kinds of work are child labourers used for in Asia and Africa?

_____

_____

_____

5

EXERCISE 71 THE WAY WE LIVE – GLOBAL PROBLEMS

Read the speech bubbles to find out what these people believe are 'world' problems.

I think that farmers in third world countries should get a better price for their products.

I think we need to plant more trees to stop all this environmental destruction.

I think we need to find a cure for some of the world's main diseases and viruses.

I think involving children in wars should not be allowed.

1. Name the issues these people are speaking about.

    a) _____

    b) _____

    c) _____

    d) _____

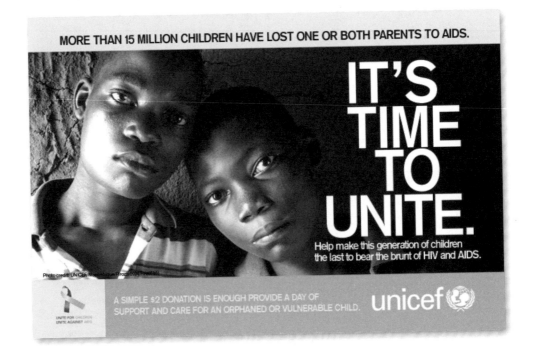

2. Can you name another global problem?

_____

_____

> The future is not a gift: it is an achievement. Every generation helps make its own future. This is the essential challenge of the present.

Robert F. Kennedy, Address to the Seattle World Fair, 1962

3. Choose any global issue and suggest two actions you could take to highlight the issue.

Issue: _____

Action 1: _____

_____

_____

_____

Action 2: _____

_____

_____

_____

EXERCISE 72 DEVELOPMENT

Look at the following bricks on the wall of development/ underdevelopment as it affects third world countries.

1. Colour the bricks **green** that you think are most important to **help** communities in the developing world to develop, and use **red** to colour the bricks that you think cause **lack of** development, or underdevelopment.

FAMINE	FAIR TRADE	PEACE	TREE PLANTING PROGRAMMES	
	SPREADING DISEASES	BUILDING A LOCAL HOSPITAL	RISING FOOD PRICES	WOMEN INVOLVED IN LOCAL DECISION-MAKING
WORLD RECESSION	MAKING SURE EVERY CHILD GOES TO SCHOOL	BUILDING TERRACES TO STOP EROSION	CONFLICT AND WAR CAUSING PEOPLE TO LEAVE THEIR HOMES	
	STOP EROSION	BUILDING A COMMUNITY WELL FOR CLEAN WATER	POOR FARMERS FORCED TO MOVE OFF THEIR LANDS BY LOGGING AND OIL COMPANIES	DEFORESTATION
CREEPING DESERTS	OVERGRAZING	PROVIDING LOANS TO POOR PEOPLE TO START BUSINESSES	DEVELOPMENT AGENCIES HELP START LONG-TERM PROJECTS IN YOUR REGION	

Adapted from *It's Not Fair: A Handbook on World Development for Youth Groups*, Christian Aid (1993)

2. What, in your opinion, are the three most important causes of underdevelopment?

   a) _____

   b) _____

   c) _____

3. What, in your opinion, are the three most important things necessary for development?

   a) _____

   b) _____

   c) _____

EXERCISE 73 AID AGENCIES

Many aid agencies are concerned with trying to help development in Third World countries by dealing with the causes of underdevelopment, such as: improving water supplies and sanitation; stopping the spread of HIV/Aids and malaria; improving agriculture; getting more children into schools; and reducing poverty by supporting community projects.

Find out more about the work of these leading aid agencies by visiting one or more of the following websites. Record your findings below.

- www.trocaire.org
- www.concern.ie
- www.goal.ie
- www.actionaid.ie
- www.gorta.ie
- www.oxfam.ie
- www.christainaid.org

1. The website I visited was _____

2. The main issues that this aid agency is concerned with are:

_____

_____

_____

_____

3. The most important new facts I found out are:

_____

_____

_____

_____

_____

4. This agency's website suggests that people can take action and help with the issues they highlight by:

_____

_____

_____

_____

_____

5. This website was interesting because:

_____

_____

_____

_____

EXERCISE 74 CAMARA

Look at the screenshot of the Camara website below and answer the questions that follow.

1. How many working computers does Camara say will be thrown out in Ireland in the next five years?

   _____

2. How many additional computers will Africa need to reach the same level of computer coverage that Ireland has today?

   _____

3. Name three things that Camara does.

   a) _____

   b) _____

   c) _____

4. How do you think the lack of access to computers and the Internet might affect development in third world countries?

    _____

    _____

    _____

    _____

5. Are there old computers being thrown out in your school or home? Check out Camara's website to see where you can bring your old computers. How could you make this the subject of an action project? Describe what you could do.

    _____

    _____

    _____

    _____

    _____

    _____

    _____

    _____

    _____

    _____

6. Which websites do you think are most useful for finding information about issues affecting developing countries? Give reasons for your answer.

    _____

    _____

    _____

EXERCISE 75 EXTRACT FROM A SPEECH BY ROBERT KENNEDY

The following is an extract from a speech by Robert F. Kennedy that he gave at the University of Cape Town, South Africa in 1962. It is known as the Day of Affirmation Address.

Robert Kennedy was the younger brother of John F. Kennedy, President of the United States. He was the youngest Attorney General in the history of the USA. He was assassinated, like his brother, while campaigning to become President of the United States.

Day of Affirmation Address

'Many of the world's greatest movements, of thought and action, have flowed from the work of a single man. A young monk began the Protestant Reformation, and a young woman reclaimed the territory of France. It was a young Italian explorer who discovered the New World, and thirty-two-year-old Thomas Jefferson who proclaimed that all men are created equal. "Give me a place to stand," said Archimedes*, "and I will move the world." These men moved the world, and so can we all. Few will have the greatness to bend history; but each of us can work to change a small portion of events, and in the total of all these acts will be written the history of this generation . . .

'Thousands of unknown men and women in Europe resisted the occupation of the Nazis and many died, but all added to the ultimate strength and freedom of their countries . . . Each time a man stands up for an ideal, or acts to improve the lot of others, or strikes out against injustice, he sends forth a tiny ripple of hope . . . those ripples build a current which can sweep down the mightiest walls of oppression and resistance.'

*Archimedes was a Greek mathematician.

1. According to this speech by Robert F. Kennedy, how have many of the world's greatest movements started?

   _____

   _____

2. Name three people Robert Kennedy uses as examples of people who have changed the world in some way.

   a) _____

   b) _____

   c) _____

3. What does Kennedy think that each person can do to help write the history of their generation?

   _____

   _____

   _____

4. According to Kennedy, how is it possible to 'send forth a tiny ripple of hope'?

   _____

   _____

   _____

5. Can you think of any other people who have helped to change the world for the better in some way?

   _____

   _____

   _____

6. Robert Kennedy's brother, John F. Kennedy, said, 'Ask not what your country can do for you, but what you can do for your country.' Do you think that this was a good message to give to citizens? Give reasons for your answer.

   _____

   _____

   _____

EXERCISE 76 REVISION

European Union Word Search

S	P	A	E	C	G	N	G	L	C	A	F	Q	B	L
A	L	Y	L	D	S	H	K	P	O	M	W	C	D	I
T	N	E	D	I	S	E	R	P	M	G	V	Z	S	C
R	H	Z	S	X	Z	J	U	O	M	B	U	T	Q	N
P	V	F	T	S	Q	K	Y	I	I	S	R	W	Q	U
H	A	F	P	E	U	P	S	Y	S	A	S	R	O	O
M	J	R	A	W	W	R	J	U	S	Q	P	H	Z	C
M	D	S	L	P	V	K	B	B	I	C	H	O	H	S
Y	K	Q	C	I	T	G	O	J	O	R	Z	E	W
A	Q	H	P	D	A	U	O	C	N	B	P	T	D	Q
T	R	J	Q	W	R	M	D	W	U	Q	O	F	S	L
L	Z	L	N	G	S	Y	E	I	T	V	P	W	X	C
L	W	S	O	Q	R	H	A	N	X	G	N	L	O	S
B	K	G	F	D	S	U	K	P	T	M	G	Z	D	E
M	O	V	F	R	R	V	M	F	D	N	O	M	E	P

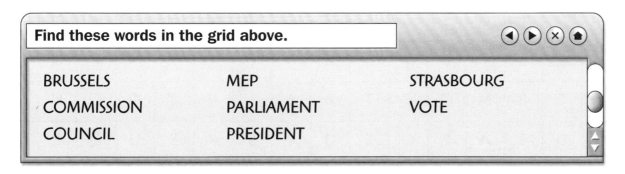

Find these words in the grid above.

BRUSSELS	MEP	STRASBOURG
COMMISSION	PARLIAMENT	VOTE
COUNCIL	PRESIDENT	

CSPE Concepts Word Search

Find the seven CSPE concepts in the word search below. ◀ ▶ ✕ ⌂

DEVELOPMENT	INTERDEPENDENCE	RIGHTS AND
LAW	STEWARDSHIP	RESPONSIBILITIES
DEMOCRACY	DIGNITY	

B	I	S	T	X	C	W	A	S	P	Q	G	T	H	P	R
I	U	R	E	M	L	J	D	H	T	I	G	H	Q	X	E
X	N	H	G	H	J	K	I	R	X	M	N	R	G	D	S
R	S	T	E	W	A	R	D	S	H	I	P	J	C	T	P
Y	T	Q	E	X	V	F	J	O	N	H	T	Q	H	X	O
T	H	E	P	R	G	F	D	S	H	X	N	G	J	B	N
I	T	S	D	G	D	I	U	Q	Y	F	I	H	I	M	S
N	O	P	E	D	N	E	D	C	U	R	Y	D	J	G	I
G	U	Y	T	R	E	W	P	Q	A	S	D	F	K	I	B
I	I	O	P	A	S	D	F	E	G	H	J	K	L	M	I
D	E	V	E	L	O	P	M	E	N	T	C	V	B	N	L
A	Q	W	E	R	T	Y	U	I	O	D	P	Z	X	A	I
S	D	F	G	Y	C	A	R	C	O	M	E	D	W	Y	T
J	L	L	T	U	I	P	H	R	T	I	P	N	F	U	I
Z	C	B	M	Q	E	T	R	A	I	P	S	G	C	H	E
F	D	S	A	P	O	E	U	Y	S	R	E	U	Q	E	S

Put each of the concepts shown in the box below into a sentence to show what it means.

1. _____

_____

2. _____

_____

3. _____

_____

4. _____

_____

5. _____

_____

6. _____

_____

7. _____

_____

LAW	INTERDEPENDENCE	HUMAN DIGNITY
RIGHTS AND RESPONSIBILITIES	STEWARDSHIP	DEVELOPMENT
	DEMOCRACY	

Sample Exam Papers

CSPE

Coimisiún na Scrúduithe Stáit
State Examinations Commission

JUNIOR CERTIFICATE EXAMINATION, 2009

CIVIC, SOCIAL AND POLITICAL EDUCATION

MONDAY, 8 JUNE – AFTERNOON 1.30 – 3.00

INSTRUCTIONS

Answer **all questions** in Section 1	(18 marks)
Answer **any three questions** in Section 2	(42 marks)
Answer **any one question** in Section 3	(20 marks)
Total	(80 marks)

SECTION 1

Answer ALL the questions in this section.

1. The following photographs are of **FOUR** human rights activists. Using the space provided, match the name of each activist with the human rights activity they are involved in.

   You may use each NAME and ACTIVITY only ONCE.

Aung San Suu Kyi	Protesting peacefully for civil rights in Burma
Nelson Mandela	Campaigning against world debt
Adi Roche	Caring for children in Chernobyl
Bono	Working for democracy in Africa

Name: _____

Activity: _____

Name: _____

Activity: _____

Name: _____

Activity: _____

Name: _____

Activity: _____

(8 marks)

2. **CSPE Course Concepts**

CSPE is based on **seven** concepts, as listed below. Beside each concept, write down one **ISSUE** or **TOPIC** that relates to that concept. You may use each issue or topic only **ONCE**.

Rights and Responsibilities: _____

Human Dignity: _____

Stewardship: _____

Development: _____

Democracy: _____

Law: _____

Interdependence: _____

(7 marks)

3. Complete each of the following sentences.

(a) Dáil Éireann and Seanad Éireann meet in L _____

H _____.

(b) A referendum is needed if the government wants to change the

C _____.

(c) Ireland has 13 elected members of the E _____

P _____.

(3 marks)

SECTION 2

Answer any THREE of the questions numbered 1, 2, 3, 4 below.
Each question carries 14 marks

1. **GIVE IT A SWIRL DAY**
Study the *Give It A Swirl Day* brochure on page 147.
When you have studied this brochure, answer the questions below.

(a) What is *Give It A Swirl Day*?

_____

Why is *Give It A Swirl Day* a special project?

_____

What are organisations encouraged to do for *Give It A Swirl Day*?

_____

(3 marks)

(b) From the brochure, name **TWO** volunteering activities that people have done.

Activity one _____

Activity two _____

(2 marks)

(c) From the brochure, give **TWO** reasons for getting involved in volunteering.

Reason one _____

Reason two _____

(2 marks)

(d) Name and describe a volunteering project (not from the list in the brochure) that **YOUR CSPE CLASS** could undertake as part of this day.

Name of Project: _____

Description: _____

_____

_____

(3 marks)

(e) In launching the Task Force on Active Citizenship, the then Taoiseach Bertie Ahern said:

'To me an active citizen is one who is aware of what is happening around them and strives towards the common good. It is about accepting a responsibility to help others and being happy to contribute to improve the quality of life of those less fortunate than ourselves.'

Do you agree with this point of view? Explain your answer.

_____

_____

_____

_____

(4 marks)

2. **Universal Declaration of Human Rights 60th Anniversary.**
    Study the UDHR @ 60 postcard on page 147.
    When you have studied the postcard, answer the questions below.

    (a) On what date did the nations of the world adopt the Universal Declaration of Human Rights?

    _____

    How many articles are in this declaration?

    _____

    What organisation is promoting this postcard campaign?

    _____

    (3 marks)

    (b) What do the thirty coloured words on the postcard refer to?

    _____

    (1 mark)

    (c) Choose two words from the thirty coloured words on the postcard and explain the right suggested by each of the two

    First Word: _____

    Explanation: _____

    Second Word: _____

    Explanation: _____

    (2 marks)

    (d) **YOUR CSPE CLASS** wants to organise an event to mark the UDHR @ 60 Anniversary.
    Describe the event and write a slogan for it.

    Description of event _____

    _____

    Slogan: _____

    (4 marks)

(e) Name and explain **TWO** actions **YOUR SCHOOL** could take to promote awareness of people whose rights are being denied.

First Action: _____

Explanation: _____

_____

_____

Second Action: _____

Explanation: _____

_____

_____

(4 marks)

3. **TIPS FROM CHANGE.IE**
Study the *Tips from Change.ie* website information on page 147.
When you have studied this information, answer the questions below.

(a) From the information on the website name **THREE** things you could do with unwanted clothes other than throwing them away.

1. _____
2. _____
3. _____

(3 marks)

What tip does the website give for old mobile phones?

_____

(1 mark)

(b) According to the website, what damage can old batteries do to the environment if they are not recycled?

_____

_____

(2 marks)

(c) 'Recycle' is one of the 3 Rs. What are the other two?

R_____

R_____

(2 marks)

(d) Name and describe **ONE** action the **DEPARTMENT OF THE ENVIRONMENT** could take to encourage people in Ireland to recycle more.

Name of Action: _____

Description: _____

_____

(3 marks)

(e) *'Over half the contents of your dustbin could be recycled or turned into compost. At present we recycle less than one quarter of our domestic waste.'*
You Can Save the Planet, Rick Hough

What message do you take from this quote?

_____

_____

_____

_____

(3 marks)

4. **The Niall Mellon Township Trust.**
Study the Niall Mellon Township Trust information leaflet on page 148.
When you have studied this information leaflet, answer the questions below.

(a) What inspired Niall Mellon to set up this Trust?

_____

In what year was the Niall Mellon Township Trust set up?

_____

What does the Niall Mellon Township Trust do?

_____

(3 marks)

(b) From your reading of the information leaflet name **THREE** challenges that poverty brings.

First challenge _____

Second challenge _____

Third challenge _____

(3 marks)

(c) Why do you think it is important for local communities to get involved in projects like the Niall Mellon Township Trust?

_____

_____

_____

(2 marks)

(d) A teacher from your school has volunteered to travel to South Africa to build houses with the Niall Mellon Township Trust. Name and describe **ONE** fundraising activity **YOUR SCHOOL** could undertake to help this teacher.

Name of activity: _____

Description: _____

_____

(2 marks)

(e) Name and describe **TWO** other actions **YOUR COMMUNITY** could take that would help make it possible for this teacher to go to South Africa.

First Action: _____

Description: _____

_____

Second Action: _____

Description: _____

_____

(4 marks)

SECTION 3
Answer ONE of the questions numbered 1, 2, 3, 4 below.
Each question carries 20 marks.

1. **School community**

   Your CSPE class has decided to produce a booklet about the school for new First Years as an Action Project that would benefit the school community.

   (a) Name and describe **THREE** groups that **YOUR CLASS** would set up in order to undertake this Action Project. (6 marks)

   (b) Name **FOUR** different things that you would include in this booklet and explain why they would help new First Years coming to your school. (8 marks)

   (c) Name and explain **TWO** skills that you would use while producing this booklet. (6 marks)

2. **Mobile phone text bullying**

   Texting is a great way to stay in touch with your friends and family but sadly it can also be used to bully, harass and frighten people. Text bullying can be texts that frighten, insult, threaten you or make you feel uncomfortable. Your CSPE class has decided to do some work on this issue.

   (a) Write a short article for your school newsletter in which you give **THREE** pieces of advice about what students should do if they receive a bullying text message. (6 marks)

   (b) Name an Action Project that **YOUR CSPE CLASS** could undertake on this issue and describe **THREE** tasks your class would do as part of this action. (8 marks)

   (c) Name and describe **THREE** other actions that **YOUR SCHOOL** could take to help prevent text bullying in your school. (6 marks)

3. **Local elections**

   It is the year of Local and European Elections in Ireland. For your Action Project your CSPE class has decided to take a closer look at the Local Elections in your area by inviting one of the candidates to talk to you.

   (a) Describe the work of **THREE** teams that your class would set up in order to undertake this Action Project. (6 marks)

   (b) Name **TWO** areas you would ask the candidate to talk about and give a reason why you have selected each of these areas. (8 marks)

   (c) Explain **THREE** reasons why it is important for Irish citizens to vote in local elections. (6 marks)

4. **CCTV (Closed Circuit Television)**

Your local town is planning to install CCTV cameras as part of a campaign to reduce crime in your area. Your CSPE class is interested in this, and has asked your teacher if you can do an Action Project about this issue.

(a) Your class has decided to have a debate on the topic, *'CCTV Reduces Crime'*, before carrying out the Action Project. Write down **ONE** argument in favour and **ONE** argument against this topic. (6 marks)

(b) Name **ONE** action that you could undertake to find out how students in your school feel about CCTV cameras. Name **TWO** committees that you would set up in order to carry out this action. After you have carried out this action, what would you do with your findings? (8 marks)

(c) Design a poster you would use to show students in your school how you feel about the CCTV cameras. As well as a drawing, your poster should include a **SLOGAN** which will show students your opinion on the use of CCTV cameras in your town. (Use page 146 of this book, which has been left blank for your drawing.) (6 marks)

Please tick [✔] the question from Section 3 that you are answering

Q. 1 ☐   **Q. 2** ☐   **Q. 3** ☐   **Q. 4** ☐

_____

_____

_____

_____

_____

_____

_____

_____

_____

_____

_____

_____

_____

_____

_____

For answering Question (c) in Section 3.

Give It A Swirl Day – Brochure for Section 2, Question 1

What is Give it a Swirl Day?
Give It A Swirl Day is the national day of volunteering. It is organised by Volunteer Centres Ireland and other partner organisations.

Give It A Swirl Day is a special project as it is about hands-on involvement rather than fundraising. This gives volunteers an immediate sense of achievement.

For Give It A Swirl Day, we ask organisations to have once-off volunteering opportunities which are good for them and the community. It also shows that volunteering, even for a few short hours, can be a lot of fun and can make a difference.

GIVE IT A SWIRL DAY
Volunteers have:

Played bingo, played cards with older people

Cleaned up school grounds, picked up litter and raked up the autumn leaves

Invited local people with a disability to an 'Activity Day' hosted by their school

Taught older people how to use their mobile phones or e-mail

Why Get Involved?
● Volunteering is fun and rewarding!

● Great way to develop new skills, team building and leadership!

● You get the chance to make a difference in your community!

● Meet new people who feel strongly about the same issues as you

● Volunteering contributes to a better work-life balance

volunteer centres
Ionad d'Obir Deonacha na hÉireann
IRELAND

UDHR@60 – Postcard for Section 2, Question 2

LIFE DIGNITY SECURITY **FREEDOM** RESPECT
JUSTICE EQUALITY **REMEDY PROTECTION**
FAIRNESS FAIR-TRIAL **RESPONSIBILITY**
WORK ASYLUM CONSCIENCE **IDENTITY**
MOVEMENT **HUMAN RIGHTS** EXPRESSION
FAMILY PARTICIPATION DEMOCRACY
SOLIDARITY LEISURE EDUCATION **PRIVACY**
WELFARE **HEALTH** CULTURE **HOME**

Website Information for Section 2, Question 3

Tips from Change.ie
(Adapted from: www.change.ie.)

Recycle. Are you tired of your old clothes? Donate them, rather than just throwing them away and clogging up our landfills. If you're handing them down to your sisters and brothers, that's great; if not, pass them along to a recognised charity.

They'll make sure they get to someone that needs them.

Or, you can swap them with friends and brighten up your wardrobe!

If you're not feeling so charitable, try selling your old clothes or accessories online or in resale shops. You'll make some money, provide someone else with a good buy and you will be helping the environment.

Recycle. And not just the normal things like paper and glass. Are you getting the new phone for your birthday? Lucky you . . . but not so lucky for your old phone. Make sure you recycle it! Same goes for used batteries . . . the materials used to make these products can damage our water supplies. Ensure they wind up in the right place to be recycled and re-used. Dispose of these either to a charity or at your local recycling centre.

The Niall Mellon Township Trust - Information Leaflet for Section 2, Question 4

When Niall Mellon saw first-hand the poverty in the townships in South Africa, he set up the Niall Mellon Township Trust in 2002 to provide homes to the poor communities in the townships. Volunteers from Ireland raise money and travel to South Africa to build houses in the townships.

- Living in a shack has been shown to have a negative impact on health, education and self-esteem.
- Without a sense of home, people's self-respect can be diminished.
- Without basic housing, families are not equipped to face the other challenges poverty brings like crime, poor education, inadequate nutrition, decaying neighbourhoods and sub-standard healthcare.

Most of the workforce comes from the townships themselves. Community development is a central part of the work of the Niall Mellon Township Trust, working with local communities in the planning and design of the new communities.

Adapted from: www.irishtownship.com

Coimisiún na Scrúduithe Stáit
State Examinations Commission

JUNIOR CERTIFICATE EXAMINATION, 2008

CIVIC, SOCIAL AND POLITICAL EDUCATION

MONDAY, 9 JUNE – AFTERNOON 1.30 – 3.00

INSTRUCTIONS

Answer **all questions** in Section 1	(18 marks)
Answer **any three questions** in Section 2	(42 marks)
Answer **any one question** in Section 3	(20 marks)
Total	(80 marks)

SECTION 1

Answer ALL of the questions in this section.

1. The photographs below are of four politicians who are, or who have been, Cabinet members in the Irish government. In the space provided, write down the name of the politician who matches each picture.

(a) Name: _____

(b) Name: _____

(c) Name: _____

(d) Name: _____

(8 marks)

2. (a) **Which one of the following people is the Secretary General of the United Nations?**

Put a tick [✔] in the box opposite the correct name.

(i) John Bruton ☐   (iii) Gordon Brown ☐

(ii) Ban Ki-Moon ☐   (iv) Jose Manuel Barroso ☐

(b) **How many Dáil constituencies are there at present?**

Put a tick [✔] in the box opposite the correct number.

(i) 13 ☐   (iii) 43 ☐

(ii) 26 ☐   (iv) 50 ☐

(c) **The European Parliament meets each month in Brussels and also in one other European city. Name the other European city.**

Put a tick [✔] in the box opposite the correct city.

(i) London ☐   (iii) Budapest ☐

(ii) Prague ☐   (iv) Strasbourg ☐

(d) In what building do the Dáil and Seanad usually meet?

Put a tick [✔] in the box opposite the correct building.

(i) The GPO ☐   (iii) Áras an Uachtaráin ☐

(ii) Stormont ☐   (iv) Leinster House ☐

(4 marks)

3. **Complete each of the following sentences.**

(a) The place where votes are cast in an election is called a p_____

s_____.

(b) A vote to change the Constitution of Ireland is called a r_____.

(c) The Deputy Prime Minister in Ireland is known as An T_____.

(d) The person who keeps order in Dáil Éireann during debates is called the

C_____ C_____.

(e) Mary Mc Aleese is the name of the P_____ of I_____.

(f) The h_____ is the national symbol of Ireland and appears on all government letters and envelopes.

(6 marks)

SECTION 2

Answer any THREE of the questions numbered 1, 2, 3, 4 below.
Each question carries 14 marks.

1. **Fairtrade**

    Study the *Fairtrade* poster on page 161.
    Above the picture of the poster you will read *Fairtrade* – Poster for Section 2, Question 1.
    When you have studied this poster, answer the questions below.

    (a) What does the Fairtrade Mark guarantee?

    _____

    According to the poster, state **TWO** things that Fairtrade means.

    First _____

    Second _____

    (3 marks)

    (b) What organisation produced this poster?

    _____

    (1 mark)

    (c) Name **TWO** Fairtrade products that you can buy in Ireland.

    First product _____

    Second product _____

    (2 marks)

    (d) Describe **TWO** actions that **YOUR CSPE CLASS** could take to promote Fairtrade products in your school.

    First Action: _____

    _____

    _____

    Second Action: _____

    _____

    _____

    (4 marks)

(e) *'Before you finish eating your breakfast this morning, you've depended on more than half the world. This is the way our universe is structured. We aren't going to have peace on earth until we recognise this basic fact.'*
(Martin Luther King)

What point do you think Martin Luther King is making in the above statement?

_____

_____

_____

_____

_____

_____

(4 marks)

2. **Ombudsman for Children**
   Study the *Ombudsman for Children* leaflet printed on page 161.
   Above the leaflet you will read *Ombudsman for Children* – Leaflet for Section 2, Question 2.
   When you have studied this leaflet, answer the questions below.

   (a) Who is the Ombudsman for Children?

   _____

   Name the Act that set up the Office of Ombudsman for Children.

   _____

   What is the aim of the Ombudsman for Children?

   _____

   _____

   (3 marks)

   (b) What are the Ombudsman's main areas of work?

   _____

   _____

   What is the email address of the Ombudsman for Children's Office?

   _____

   (2 marks)

(c) The UN passed a Convention on the Rights of the Child in 1989 in order to give extra protection to children. Name **THREE** of these rights.

First Right _____

Second Right _____

Third Right _____

(3 marks)

(d) Name **TWO** actions that **YOUR SCHOOL** could take in order to hear the opinions of students.

First Action: _____

Second Action: _____

(2 marks)

(e) Ireland signed the UN Convention in September 1992 and must hear the voices of children and young people. Describe **TWO** activities that the **IRISH GOVERNMENT** could organise to make sure that the voices and opinions of young people are heard.

First Activity _____

_____

_____

_____

Second Activity _____

_____

_____

_____

(4 marks)

3. **Bin It Campaign**
   Study the *Bin It Campaign* webpage printed on page 162.
   Above the picture of the web page you will read *Bin It Campaign* – Web page for Section 2, Question 3.
   When you have studied this web page, answer the questions below.

   (a) What environmental problem is this website about?

   _____

   What is the website address?

   _____

What is the purpose of the UK and Eire survey?

_____

(3 marks)

(b) This web page promotes **THREE** steps for all responsible users of chewing gum. What are they?

(i) _____ **(ii)** _____ **(iii)** _____

(3 marks)

(c) Apart from litter on our streets, name **TWO** other environmental problems in Ireland.

First Problem _____

Second Problem _____

(2 marks)

(d) Name **TWO** actions your **CSPE CLASS** could take to help reduce litter in your school.

First Action: _____

Second Action: _____

(2 marks)

(e) Name and explain **TWO** actions that the **GOVERNMENT** could take to help reduce the problem of litter in Ireland.
You must not use any of the actions you have mentioned already.

First Action: _____

Explanation: _____

_____

_____

Second Action: _____

Explanation: _____

_____

_____

(4 marks)

4. **Self Help in Gogne, Eritrea**
   Study the *Self Help in Gogne, Eritrea* newsletter article printed on page 162.
   Above the article you will read *Self Help in Gogne, Eritrea* – Newsletter
   Article for Section 2, Question 4.
   When you have studied the newsletter article, answer the questions below.

   (a) What Irish organisation carried out the project in Gogne?

   _____

   According to the newsletter article, how many people live in Gogne?

   _____

   (2 marks)

   (b) What was the problem for the people of Gogne?

   _____

   What did the project do with the help of the people?

   _____

   Why did the success of the project change the price of water?

   _____

   _____

   (4 marks)

   (c) Name **TWO** other Irish organisations that work with communities in the
   Developing World.

   First Organisation _____

   Second Organisation _____

   (2 marks)

   (d) For many years Bono and Bob Geldof have asked world governments to
   cancel debt in Developing Countries. Why are they asking world governments
   to do this?

   _____

   _____

   _____

   _____

   (2 marks)

(e) Apart from fundraising, suggest **TWO** actions that **YOUR CSPE CLASS** could take to help a community in the Developing World.

First Action: _____

_____

_____

_____

Second Action: _____

_____

_____

_____

(4 marks)

SECTION 3

Answer ONE of the questions numbered 1, 2, 3, 4 below.
Each question carries 20 marks.
Page 160 has been left blank for the poster/invitation questions.

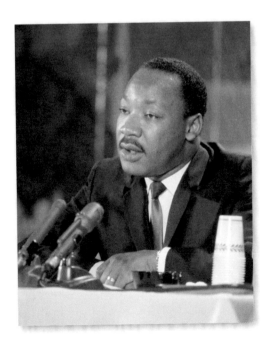

1. **40th Anniversary of the Death of Martin Luther King**

Martin Luther King was assassinated in Memphis, Tennessee on 4 April 1968. He is famous for his human rights work for black people in the USA. Your CSPE class has decided to organise a talk from a guest speaker to mark the 40th anniversary of Martin Luther King's death.

(a) Design an invitation you would send to parents and members of your community inviting them to this talk. In your invitation you should include at least **THREE** pieces of information that parents and people in your community will need to know.

(A blank page for you to draw up the invitation has been included on page 160 of this book.)

(6 marks)

(b) Name THREE groups that your CSPE class would have to set up in order to organise this event. Describe in detail the work of each of these groups.

(6 marks)

(c) Write an article for your school magazine explaining why it is important for students to support this event. Your article should include at least **THREE** reasons.

(8 marks)

2. **International Women's Day**
International Women's Day is celebrated on 8 March every year. Your CSPE class has decided to celebrate International Women's Day.

(a) Write a short speech for a school assembly explaining why it is important to celebrate International Women's Day. You should give **TWO** reasons why your class thinks this is important.

(6 marks)

(b) **Design a poster:** Your class wishes that all students will take part in the International Women's Day celebrations and has decided to design a poster for display in your school. Write down **THREE** key pieces of information that you would use in this poster and design the poster in the blank space on page 160.

(6 marks)

(c) Describe **THREE** tasks your CSPE class would have to undertake in order to organise and run your International Women's Day celebration.

(8 marks)

3. **New Motorway**
The National Roads Authority (NRA) has announced that a new motorway is to be built. The route chosen crosses an area where important wildlife will be threatened. You and members of your community have decided to campaign for a different route for the new motorway.

(a) Write a letter to your local Councillor objecting to the planned route through this important environmental area. In your letter make **THREE** arguments against the route that has been chosen.

(6 marks)

(b) Apart from letter writing, describe **THREE** actions your community could take as part of the campaign to get a different route for the motorway.

(6 marks)

(c) Name and explain **TWO** skills that you would use while campaigning against the proposed motorway development.

(8 marks)

4. **International Year of Planet Earth**

2008 is UN International Year of Planet Earth. The UN hopes to raise awareness about climate change and sustainable development. Your CSPE class has decided to develop a website to raise awareness about these issues.

(a) Name **TWO** environmental organisations that your CSPE class would contact to help you develop your understanding of climate change. Explain why you have chosen these organisations. (6 marks)

(b) Climate change is linked to sustainable development, which makes sure that people using the earth's resources today do not limit their use by people in the future. Describe **THREE** things you would put on your website showing what people could do to use the earth's resources more carefully today.
(6 marks)

(c) Write an introduction for the homepage of your website. Include a slogan and **TWO** other pieces of information about the problems facing Planet Earth today. (8 marks)

Please tick [✔] the question from Section 3 that you are answering

Q. 1 ☐   Q. 2 ☐   Q. 3 ☐   Q. 4 ☐

_____

_____

_____

_____

_____

_____

_____

_____

_____

_____

_____

_____

_____

_____

For answering the POSTER/INVITATION Questions in Section 3.

1. (a)

2. (b)

Fairtrade – **Poster for Section 2, Question 1**

FAIRTRADE
Guarantees
a **better deal**
for Third World
Producers

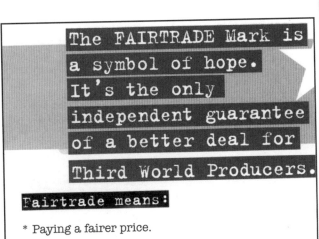

The FAIRTRADE Mark is a symbol of hope. It's the only independent guarantee of a better deal for Third World Producers.

Fairtrade means:

* Paying a fairer price.
* Buying directly from producers.
* Paying a bonus on top of the minimum price to enable community development.
* Trading on a long term basis, enabling producers to plan for the future.

  www.oxfamireland.org

Ombudsman for Children – **Leaflet for Section 2, Question 2**

Who is the Ombusdman for Children?
Emily Logan is the first Ombudsman for Children in Ireland.

Emily worked as a children's nurse for 22 years before she became Ombudsman for Children, so she has lots of experience of working with children and young people.

What does the Ombudsman for Children do?
The Ombudsman for Children's Office was set up under the Ombudsman for Children's Act, 2002. The aim of the Ombudsman for Children is to promote and protect the rights and interests of children and young people under the age of 18.

The Ombudsman for Children Act, 2002, describes in detail what the Ombudsman for Children can do. The three main areas of work outlined in the Ombudsman for Children Act, 2002 are:
● Promoting children's rights
● Research and policy
● Complaints and investigations

Ombudsman
for children and young people

Write to us at:
Ombudsman for Children's Office
Millennium House
52-56 Great Strand Street
Dublin 1

or e-mail us at oco@oco.ie
or ring us on Lo-Call 1890 654 654
or (01) 865 6800

Bin It Campaign – Web page for Section 2, Question 3

Self Help in Gogne, Eritrea – Newsletter Article for Section 2, Question 4

⟲ Self Help

Newsletter Article: Gogne Water Problems Solved

Self Help is an Irish organisation working in Africa. Recently it carried out a project with the help of the people in the town of Gogne in Eritrea. Life was becoming more and more difficult for the 15,000 people who lived in the town because they were very short of water.

Clean water was being sold by traders at the very high price of 40 nakfa a barrel (€1.80). After a few months the *Self Help* project decided to put a generator and pump into the town's main water spring. This made public water available again at the much lower cost of 5 nakfa a barrel (€0.25 cents). The project also repaired and updated many of the local fountains and taps.

Four public fountains around the town were repaired and at once the water began to flow again. This has made a big difference to the people of Gogne.

*(Adapted from **Self Help** Newsletter 2007)*

ACKNOWLEDGMENTS

The authors would like to acknowledge the help and advice given by the following:

80:20, ActionAid, Afri, ALONE, Amnesty International, ARASI (Association of Refugees and Asylum Seekers Ireland), Senator Ivana Bacik, Ballymun Partnership, Barnardos, John Byrne, Camara, Ann Carroll, Childnet International, Christian Aid, Citizen Traveller, *Clare Companion*, Tom Clonan, Coalition to Stop Child Soldiers, Combat Poverty, Concern Worldwide, Council for People with Disabilities, Courts Service of Ireland, Brian Crowley MEP, Dáil na nÓg, Councillor Clare Daly, DEFY, Detective Garda Cathal Delaney, Department of the Environment, Department of Justice, Equality and Law Reform, Department of An Taoiseach, Proinsias De Rossa MEP, Shane Doyle and Gorey Skate Club, Dublin Simon Community, Clare Dunne, ECO UNESCO, ENFO, Equality Authority, Fairtrade Mark Ireland, Fianna Fáil, Fine Gael, Focus Ireland, Foróige, Free the Children, Peter Gaynor, GOAL, GoodWeave, Green Party, Ciaran Halford, Holocaust Educational Trust of Ireland, Irene Hughes and Ashbourne Community School students and Green School Committee members, International Labour Office, Councillor Kealin Ireland, Irish Aid, *Irish Examiner*, Irish Fair Trade Network, *Irish Independent*, Irish Red Cross, *Irish Times*, Irish Traveller Movement, ISPCA, Nellie Joyce, Kick it Out, Craig Kielburger, Labour Party, *LifeTimes*, Local Planet, Longford County Council, Grant Masterson, Mairead McGuinness MEP, MiCandidate, Catherine Murnane, Margaret Murphy, National Children's Office, National Youth Council of Ireland, NewsFour, Senator David Norris, Caoimhghín Ó Caoláin TD, Anne O'Donnell, Office of the Minister of Children and Youth Affairs, Offices of the European Parliament, Ombudsman for Children, Outreach International, Oxfam, Pavee Point, Pride of Place: Co-operation Ireland, Councillor John Ryan, Trevor Sargent TD, Save Tara/Skryne Valley Group, Sinn Féin, Socialist Party, SpunOut, Sustainable Energy Ireland, An Taisce, Trócaire, Trust, UNICEF, United Nations High Commission for Refugees (Ireland), URBAN Ballyfermot, Vincentian Partnership for Social Justice, Mark Waddock, Jake Walsh (Tipperary South Comhairle na nÓg), *Western People*, *Wexford Echo*, Wicklow County Council, World Development Movement.

For permission to reproduce extracts, the authors are grateful to the following:
Adrian Mitchell for his poem 'Back in the Playground Blues' and Jacqueline Wilson for her novel *Secrets*.

The authors extend their thanks to the teachers and students of Killinarden Community School, Tallaght and Loreto College, St Stephen's Green.

Jeanne Barrett would like to dedicate this edition of *Impact!* to the memory of her mother Nance Barrett.